Why Can't You Just Give Me the Number?

Why Can't You Just Give Me the Number?

An Executive's Guide to Using Probabilistic
Thinking to Manage Risk and Make Better
Decisions

by Patrick Leach

Probabilistic Publishing

Editors: Dave and Debbie Charlesworth

Initial printing: September, 2006
Second printing: February, 2010

Probabilistic Publishing

Florida:
352-338-1789

Texas:
1702 Hodge Lake Ln
Sugar Land, TX 77478
281-277-4006
www.decisions-books.com
e-mail: dave@decisions-books.com

Written, designed, and printed in the United States of America.

Library of Congress Control Number: 2006933143

ISBN: 0-9647938-5-7
ISBN 13: 978-0-9647938-5-9

To my wife Becky:
I'm lucky and proud to have you by my side.

Acknowledgements

Many of the charts and graphs in this book were generated using Crystal Ball® Monte Carlo simulation software. I would like to thank Decisioneering Inc. for allowing me to use these images and some of the concepts expressed in their training workbook. I have also used Treeage DATA to create some of the decision trees that appear in this book. If any of these figures or ideas are misrepresented in this book or otherwise present ideas that prove to be incorrect, the errors are mine, not Decisioneering's or Treeage's.

In addition to the books listed in the bibliography, I would like to note the January 2006 issue of the *Harvard Business Review*. This issue was dedicated to ideas, research studies, and problems surrounding decision making, and I have cited several articles from it. It is well worth reading.

I need to thank Rick Omlor for his valuable feedback on the first draft. It is a better book for his comments and suggestions. I also want to acknowledge Gary Bush, Fred Gibson, Bill Haskett, and Bob Ameo for their detailed and insightful input, Steve Anderson for his help on Chapter 10, Lisa Eisele and Rob Brown for their contributions and thoughts, and Jerry Lieberman for his marvelous anecdotes. To the rest of my colleagues who gave me the benefit of their experiences but whose stories I did not include, I apologize – I couldn't use them all, and I truly appreciate your thoughtfulness.

To Dave and Debbie Charlesworth, my editors and publishers, many thanks. Your suggestions undoubtedly made the book much more readable, entertaining, and interesting. You deserve a fair amount of the credit.

And I owe a special debt of gratitude to Jim Murtha, who clarified many subtle mathematical distinctions, forced me to be more rigorous in my terms and definitions, and helped me to explain some of the key ideas more clearly. If the reader has any problems understanding these concepts, it will undoubtedly be in those areas of the book where I strayed from Jim's advice.

I am also very thankful for my wife Becky, who encouraged me as I wrote and rewrote the manuscript. I could not have completed this book without her.

Note

There are a number of legitimate perspectives on how best to deal with uncertainty in business. The points made and the issues raised in this book are intended to provoke discussion. We welcome your thoughts, feedback, anecdotes, and comments.

We are very appreciative of the positive reception this book has received. Frank Koch (Chevron) deserves our heartfelt thanks for characterizing this book as "the book I wish I had written" and recommending it so articulately. We'd also like to thank Jim Franklin (Oracle) for his continuing efforts to promote the book among his colleagues.

Patrick Leach   pat.leach@entouch.net
Dave Charlesworth   dave@decisions-books.com

Contents

"I shall never believe that God plays dice with the world."
– Albert Einstein

"Stop telling God what to do."
– Niels Bohr

1

Why Can't You Just Give Me the Number?

Mike Sexton, co-host of television's World Poker Tour and a professional poker player, once commented that all players at the final table in a tournament know the odds, i.e., they all can quickly estimate the probabilities of the various possible outcomes, given what they know about their own cards and the common cards. Anyone who cannot do this won't make it a week into the tournament, let alone get all the way to the final table. What separates a great player from the rest are his (or her) other skills, specifically the ability to "read" other players to tell when they're bluffing and to prevent others from reading him.

Knowing the probabilities just gets you into the game; in order to win, you need additional skills.

Ironically, the reverse is often true in business – the players have the skills but do not understand the odds. Most executives and managers are intelligent and highly skilled in-

Endeavor	Gets One Into the Game	Gives Competitive Advantage	Needed to Win
Poker	Knowing the Odds	Skills	BOTH
Business	Skills	Knowing the Odds	BOTH

Table 1.1. Odds and Skills

dividuals with a good sense for the industries in which they operate. However, competitors are also led by bright and capable people. Some are certainly more capable than others, but most companies employ talented and intelligent managers and executives. In business, having the skills just gets you into the game (Table 1.1).

But how many executives really know the odds? How many require rigorous assessment of the probabilities associated with the myriad possible outcomes of their actions, their competitors' actions, the market's actions, the government's actions, potential new competitors with new technology, etc., and then consistently incorporate these assessments into their decision-making process? Granted, this is more difficult than calculating the odds of winning a hand of poker, but that's no excuse. The tools and methodologies for such analyses have existed for years, and imperfect though they may be, proper use of them will yield valuable insights into one's business. Those who understand and employ these methods have no guarantee of superior results every time, but they will certainly improve their odds. In the long run (as in poker), competitors who have both skills and a good understanding of the probabilities will outperform those who don't.

In business today, managerial ranks are filled with dedicated and intelligent individuals who — despite their talents — have no real idea of the probabilities of success or failure associated with the alternative courses of action available to them. An executive who possesses the same skills, but who also uses quantitative analysis of these probabilities, understands the results, and incorporates this thinking into his or her decision-making process will ultimately enjoy a competitive advantage.

Market leaders as diverse as Harrah's, Capital One, Amazon, Wal-Mart, Progressive Insurance, and Marriott regularly use statistical analysis, quantitative modeling, and optimization to outperform peers.[1]

Of course, most executives have no desire to perform probabilistic calculations themselves. That's what analysts are for. This book is *not* designed give you the ins and outs of statistical methods, or show you how to calculate the standard deviation of a set of data, or enable you to create efficient frontier charts for your portfolio of opportunities. This is *not* an instruction manual for hands-on statistical analysis; there are a number of excellent books of that type already on the market.

This is an overview of the world of probabilistic methodology – or rather, the view from a senior manager's perspective. We'll occasionally work with numbers and terminology, but the idea is not to turn you into a statistician or an economic model builder. My purpose is (1) to convince you of the importance of using probabilistic thinking as part of your decision making process, and (2) to give you the foundation you'll need to interpret the results of statistical analyses appropriately. If you already have a good fundamental understanding of probabilistic methods, the individual chapters can function as references on specific topics. There are tricks to know and traps to avoid in many areas of business when applying probabilistic thinking.

Let's return to the poker analogy for a moment. In poker, as in business, sometimes you get better cards than your opponents and sometimes your cards are inferior – and a good player will sometimes win with weaker cards than those held by his opponent. Unlike chess (in which both players have access to all the information they need to make optimal decisions), in poker you are constantly expected to make decisions with only a fraction of the total existing information. The same is true in business. Over the long haul, a superior poker player will usually beat a weaker one, but on any given hand, the better player might lose (often through no fault of his own). Also, the superior player has to have enough chips to hang in there long enough for statistics to kick in. Being a better player doesn't guarantee that you'll win every pot – it just improves your odds.

Professional poker players know this, of course, and plan their play accordingly. They know that they cannot guarantee good outcomes; the best they can do is to make good decisions as often as possible. Sometimes this results in calling your opponent's bluff when you're holding a king-high straight, only to discover that your opponent holds a full house and wasn't bluffing at all. Good players learn to shrug these disappointments off, recognizing that the decision was the right one, even if losing more money was the result.

Likewise, we cannot guarantee good results on every project in business. The best we can do is to make good decisions consistently. And we simply cannot do this if we don't know the odds – i.e., the probabilities associated with the various possible outcomes.

I became aware of the need for this book while teaching industry workshops in risk management, Monte Carlo modeling, and probabilistic methodology. A distressingly large number of the technical professionals in my classes would say something along the lines of, "This is all great stuff, but until my boss can understand what I'm doing – at least on a macro level – it's almost a waste of time. He's not going to incorporate probabilistic information into his decisions because he doesn't trust it. And he doesn't trust it because he doesn't understand it." The title of this book comes from the phrase these men and women heard so often after showing their bosses the results of probabilistic analyses.

Some of their quotes were gems. One engineer told of a project manager who said, "We don't have enough information to give ranges of possible values for costs. We'll have to

DEFINITIONS

Deterministic:

> Using single values for each input parameter and generating single values for each output calculation. This is the way most spreadsheets work.

Probabilistic (also called Stochastic, and often called Monte Carlo):

> Using a range of values and associated probabilities for each input parameter (usually given as a probability function), and generating a histogram of values for each output calculation (sometimes called an output probability distribution).

make our best estimates and model it deterministically." The engineer tried to tell him that when data is sparse and uncertainty is high, that's the *best* time to model things probabilistically, but to no avail.

Obviously, there is a fundamental lack of understanding here. This book supplies that understanding. I have intentionally kept it brief. I have included charts and graphs where they help to explain a concept. When it comes to statistics, a picture is sometimes worth a thousand numbers.

We will cover concepts and terms which may be unfamiliar to you. As such, I have placed definitions at the beginning of subsequent chapters as needed, and there is a glossary in the back. Some definitions are unambiguous and can be found in any statistics text. Some definitions are topics of debate among people who perform probabilistic analyses for a living. When I'm dealing with the latter type, I've given the definition that will be used in this book.

I have also included anecdotes as sidebars to emphasize some key points. Except for the "Shell Game" brain teaser in the appendix, these are all true stories with names omitted or changed to preserve anonymity. I think you'll enjoy them and – more importantly – I hope you'll remember them. The lessons learned by the companies in these stories drive home the point that – as in poker – long-term success in business requires both skill *and* knowledge of the odds.

Endnotes

1. Davenport, Thomas H. "Competing on Analytics." *Harvard Business Review*, Vol. 84, No. 1, pp. 98-107, January 2006.

*"What is a cynic? A man who knows the price of everything,
and the value of nothing."*
— Oscar Wilde

2

The Root of All Value

In this chapter, I make the case that all value generated by business executives comes – directly or indirectly – from how they manage uncertainty. Without uncertainty, a share of a company's stock is effectively a bond, with guaranteed future cash flows. Guaranteed bonds don't need management. But stocks (or rather, companies issuing stock) certainly do.

DEFINITIONS

Uncertainty:

For the purposes of this book, an uncertainty is a parameter or measurement the value of which we do not know, and cannot know until some time in the future (if we can find out the value by looking it up or asking somebody, it's a fact or a given which is not yet known to us, not an uncertainty). Examples would be how many widgets we'll sell next year, how much electricity our new plant will use next month, or what the snowfall in Colorado will be this winter. We usually characterize uncertainties with an estimate of the range of values we believe the parameter could have, plus a probability distribution to show how likely we believe the various values in that range to be.

Probability Distribution:

A curve or histogram showing the range of possible values for the parameter in question along the x-axis and the probability of occurrence (or relative probability of occurrence) along the y-axis. The best-known example is the Gaussian distribution, also known as the Normal distribution or "bell curve."

Note that in this book, the term, "distribution," generally refers to *output* distributions – that is, distributions that are created by one algorithm or another in a Monte Carlo simulation model. As managers, these are the distributions with which you will generally be dealing. Output distributions are histograms. Input distributions – those that are created by the modeler to characterize the uncertainty of the input parameters – are usually mathematical functions, not histograms, and much of what is said here does not accurately apply to them.

Risk:

Where I have used the term, "risk," as a noun, I mean the probability of loss times the potential magnitude of that loss. Where I have used it as a verb, I mean to take a chance; to put oneself in a position in which there is some probability of loss. Unfortunately, the definition of risk varies from industry to industry, and even from company to company. In the finance world, the most common definition of risk is beta, the correlation over time between an asset's value and the value of the portfolio of all possible investments (stocks, bonds, real estate, precious metals – everything). The lower the correlation, the more the asset will reduce the volatility of your portfolio, thereby reducing the "risk" of that portfolio (although this also reduces the upside potential).

Some industries simply equate risk with volatility – that is, the risk of any project is represented by the standard deviation of the measure of value. The more certain the return on investment, the less risky it is.

Others consider the amount of capital that might be lost if an investment or project goes badly to be the "risk" of that venture.

Still others use "risk" to refer to variables that have discrete success or failure outcomes (what is the risk that we will lose this lawsuit?), as opposed to variables that can have a range of values (how high might the damages be if we lose the lawsuit?). The former are called "risk variables" or "chance variables;" the latter are called "range variables" or uncertainties.

With all these different definitions, the result can be confusing, especially when "risk" is used in place of "volatility" or "uncertainty." Unfortunately, there simply is no single definition of "risk" I can give that will apply universally. Just make sure that within your own company, everyone agrees on a common definition.

Uncertainty as a Source of Value

What is the source of value in business? What enables companies to deliver value to their shareholders? I'm looking for something very fundamental here: a basic element of all business, from which successful companies derive the value that they deliver to shareholders.

When I ask this question in courses and workshops, I get a variety of answers (and a few people are usually annoyed by the apparent vagueness of the question). No one ever comes up with the answer I'm looking for: *uncertainty*. Uncertainty (I state with all the assurance of a television evangelist) is the ultimate source of value in business.

I'm usually greeted with something between blank stares and outright disbelief when I start to explain this in my classes. Nonsense, they protest – we spend a lot of time, money, and effort trying to get *rid* of uncertainty. How can it possibly be a source of value, let alone *the* source of value?

At this point, I have to concede that saying uncertainty is the source of value in business is somewhat like saying that disease and injury are the sources of value in medicine, or that crime is the source of value in police work. This is true in the sense that medicine has value because of the existence of disease and injuries, and police work has value because of the existence of crime. Without disease and injury, we would not need doctors. If there were no crimes to prevent or solve, we would not need policemen. In a similar fashion, without uncertainty, we would not need business managers.

Businesses add value because of the existence of uncertainty. The investing public is generally risk-averse when it comes to returns on their investments; this is why stocks with an expected free cash flow of X sell for less than bonds with an identical free cash flow, and bonds sell for less than comparable T-bills. Paying less up front and receiving (on average) the same cash flows means that the stock investor gets a higher return on her money than the bond investor, who gets a higher return than the T-bill investor. This is why the S&P 500 outperforms T-bills over the long haul.

But taking this to its logical conclusion means that the only way businesses can deliver higher returns to their owners is by taking capital from the risk-averse public (or risk-averse private individuals, for non-public companies), finding individual investment opportunities with significant upside potential – and significant uncertainty – and then managing these investments in such a way as to reduce overall portfolio risk to a level that is acceptable to shareholders. The specific strategies may differ from situation to situation and from company to company, but ultimately every business is trying to invest in uncertain projects and opportunities, and then deliver to owners – with some degree of certainty – a stream of free cash flows that equals or exceeds what is expected. In *Against the Gods: The Remarkable Story of Risk*, Peter Bernstein makes an impressive argument that capitalism and the free market as we know it today exist only because of the discovery of probability theory and its application to risk management.

Still skeptical? Let us consider several questions. How is value delivered to shareholders? How do we measure it? Generally, it's the after-tax return on investment that most share-holders are interested in. So where does that come from?

Higher stock prices, anticipated dividends, etc. – all stem from one thing: expected future free cash flows.* If you could somehow wave a magic wand and remove *all* uncertainty from your business, what rate of return could you deliver to your shareholders? And I don't mean the one-off bonanza that would be realized by your current investors, who bought your stock during a period of uncertainty and were lucky enough to hold it when your magic wand did its thing. I mean over the long haul, to those investors who, say, buy your shares on the open market a year from now – what rate of return could you deliver to these investors?

I submit that you could deliver the risk-free rate to these shareholders – nothing more. Anything greater than that, and an arbitrage opportunity would present itself in the market: people could borrow at the risk-free rate, buy your stock, and make a sure-fire profit (remember, your future cash flows are certain from now on).

Now, I'm not a blind believer in the free market as the answer to every problem facing humankind today, but one thing the free market is extremely good at is eliminating arbitrage opportunities (or at least making them very short-lived). With future cash flows certain, a share of your stock essentially becomes a bond, and would be priced the way bonds are priced: the present value of the cash flow discounted at the appropriate rate (in this case, the risk-free rate). There-fore, the price of your stock would quickly rise (there's that boon to the current shareholders) to the point where it equals

*The Tech Bubble

Occasionally, the investing public seems to lose its collective head when it comes to valuing stocks, as it did in the tech bubble of the late 1990s when stock prices for many companies rose to levels that were completely unsupportable by any sane projection of cash flows. The ensuing crash showed once again that even in a "new economy," real value comes only from having a realistic chance of getting more money out of an investment than one put into it.

the present value of your future free cash flows, discounted at the risk-free rate. And that risk-free rate is exactly what your shareholders would realize when those cash flows materialized.

The only thing that allows businesses to provide rates of return greater than the risk-free rate to their shareholders – the only thing that allows them to provide greater *value* – is uncertainty.* Granted, the uncertainty itself doesn't add the value; rather, it's how we manage it. But if you don't understand it, you can't manage it. *The second-most important value-adding activity a senior executive can engage in is to identify, characterize, and understand the key uncertainties in her business, and then consistently incorporate this understanding into her decisions.* (The *most* important value-adding activity for an executive is to create a corporate culture in which all employees – from the CEO to the lowest-ranking individual – are encouraged to think creatively about their jobs, their company, and their industry, and to voice their thoughts without fear of adverse reaction. But that's a subject for another book.)

To some extent, business leaders have been aware of this for decades; after all, making decisions in the face of uncertainty is a large part of what they do (especially when they are deciding upon strategy). These are intelligent men and women who work hard to understand their industries, including inherent risks. It's hardly news to them that they should consider the upsides, downsides, and probabilities associated with the likely outcomes of their decisions.

*Adding Value

Value is obviously also added by skilled professionals taking raw materials, data, or information, and applying their skills so as to create something of greater value. Examples might be a glass blower converting sand into a beautiful lamp, a scientist conducting experiments and discovering a better pain reliever, or a travel agent sifting through available options to put together a pleasant vacation. What I'm talking about here is how *business managers* add value, and what it is about business and industry that enables good managers to add value.

In recent years, though, an ever-increasing number of executives and managers are going further. They are adopting a more rigorous approach to understanding these risks and uncertainties. They're not performing the probabilistic modeling themselves, but they are familiarizing themselves with the concepts so they can interpret the results of such analyses and glean insight – often non-intuitive insight – into their situations and business opportunities.

Those who are taking this approach are gaining competitive advantage for themselves, their companies, and their shareholders.

Points to Ponder

Free-market capitalism has consistently outperformed state-run economies in terms of economic growth and value creation.

♦ How might the greater uncertainty inherent in the free-market system contribute to the higher rate of value creation?
♦ What other factors also contribute to the higher rate of value creation in free-market economies?
♦ What are the trade-offs between free-market and state-run economies, especially considering uncertainty?

Environmental Remediation

A major manufacturing company was working on an environmental remediation project. One of the environmental specialists observed that there was no way to do a probabilistic analysis because there was so much that was still unknown about the situation. The uncertainty surrounding the cost of remediation was simply too wide for the analysis to provide any real insights or have any significant value.

My colleague asked a simple question: Could the cost of the clean-up be more than $100 billion? The answer immediately came back, "No." This was a relatively small chemical spill, nothing close to the size that would trigger Superfund action.

More than $1 billion? No. $100 million? No. $10 million? Yes – almost certainly, the cost would exceed $10 million. Within five minutes, the range of uncertainty for the cost of the clean-up had been bracketed to somewhere between $10 million and $50 million – a wide range, to be sure, but less than one order of magnitude. Later in the analysis, they conducted a more rigorous assessment of the range of the cost uncertainty (and other uncertainties, too), but for now, the point had been made. Even when uncertainty is high, we can estimate a reasonable range that will help us to characterize the situation appropriately and to make a good decision.

"Doubt is an unpleasant condition, but certainty is an absurd one."
– Francois Marie Arouet, a.k.a. Voltaire

"To be absolutely certain about something, one must know everything or nothing about it."
– Olin Miller

3

Dealing with an Uncertain World

Businesses have been dealing with uncertainty for centuries. Many of the methods used were as good as the analytical capabilities of the time permitted. Others resulted from a lack of understanding of statistical principles and weren't appropriate, even at the time. In this chapter, we delve into a few of these methods in some detail and explain why they are simply inadequate today.

DEFINITION

p_{10} / p_{50} / p_{90}

The values corresponding to the 10th, 50th, and 90th percentiles, respectively, of a probability distribution. Just as your child's SAT percentile of 87 means that she did better than 87% of all the students who took the test, so the p_{33} value of a distribution means that 33% of all the possible values lie below the given number (and, conversely, 67% lie above it).

Some industries and/or some companies use the reverse convention – i.e., the term "p_{90}" is used to represent the value you have a 90% probability of *exceeding*, or 90% *confidence* that you will achieve or exceed. This can be confusing, and some people become very passionate about which approach is correct. Remember, it's just a convention; as long as everyone is speaking the same language, there's no great advantage to using one versus the other.

For the purposes of this book, "p_{90}" shall be the 90th percentile, i.e., 90% of the values lie *below* this number.

Most businessmen and businesswomen realize the importance of understanding the upside potential and downside risk associated with the opportunities and projects that their companies are working on. So what do they do about it?

Not so long ago (and still today in many companies), there were three ways that uncertainty was typically handled:[1]

- ◆ it was ignored,
- ◆ what-ifs were examined, or
- ◆ high-medium-low cases (or +/– 10% sensitivity analyses) were considered.

Each of these approaches has its problems.

If We Ignore Uncertainty, Will it Go Away?

In many cases, businesses simply ignore uncertainty. They develop their best estimates for every input parameter (sales growth, commodity prices, future market share, etc.) and calculate some measurement of value (revenue, the Net

Present Value (NPV) of a project, or maybe the purchase price of an acquisition target), assuming that the project will be successful.

The one thing you can bet good money on is that the "answer" will be wrong. Oh, it may be close – and if it's close enough, who cares? But the question is how far off the answer will be, not *whether* it will be off. The odds against guessing next year's widget sales to the last dollar are so astronomical as to be unworthy of consideration.

Yet many companies do this. I recently had a team manager tell me that he prefers to evaluate his projects deterministically (i.e. without considering uncertainty or risk) because, "either you're right or you're wrong – and if you're good, you'll be right!" Well, not necessarily. If your business is a fairly complex one, you and your team can be very good at your jobs, forecast your individual results accurately, and still miss your overall goal (see the sidebar story, "Failing to Meet Specifications").

A bigger problem with the deterministic approach is that once a value is generated, put down on paper, and incorporated into the business plan, it becomes gospel. Nobody questions it anymore; it's in the plan, so it must be true (or at the very least, it's the best estimate we have). The deterministic approach *leads to complacency*. We actually begin to believe the numbers we've generated, conveniently forgetting how shaky the initial estimates of many of the input parameters were (people also start sandbagging their forecasts to improve the probability of meeting their targets). This is dangerous, except in stable, highly predictable environments – and I know of very few businesses that operate in such a stable environment. In fact, with global markets freer and more chaotic today than at anytime in the past 75 years, rare indeed is the business without significant uncertainty.

Failing to Meet Specifications

A major manufacturer of military vehicles had a problem. Whenever a new vehicle was under development, a number of design specifications would be established beforehand (acceleration, fuel economy, cargo space, etc.). For as far back as anyone could remember, the company had never managed to meet all of the specifications in a final product.

An investigation into the matter quickly determined what the problem was not: it was not that the design engineers didn't know their jobs. These were men and women with years of experience, and they knew very well what could and could not be done. This is not to say that there was no uncertainty in their jobs; far from it. The world is full of unpleasant surprises when one moves from the drafting table to the prototype. But when they said they were 95% confident that they could design, say, an engine with X horsepower and a maximum weight of Y, then ninety-five times out of a hundred, they could.

The problem was that a typical new vehicle has thousands of individual parts. If every engineer is 95% confident about meeting the specifications on each part, that means that about 50 parts out of each 1000 aren't going to meet the specs. Maybe the engine has to be 20 pounds heavier than specified in order to produce the desired torque; maybe the chassis has to be 10 pounds heavier in order to support the engine and carry the desired amount of cargo. This extra weight then prevents the vehicle from achieving the desired acceleration. It only takes a few sub-spec parts to make the overall vehicle sub-spec.

This is a critical point, and it is analogous to many business situations. The world is full of companies that miss their targets more often than not, and don't understand why. Most of the time, there are numerous factors that contribute to the overall effort, and every one of these factors has some uncertainty associated with it. We may be justified in having a high degree of confidence that any individual factor will turn out favorably, but when they are all taken together, the probability of overall success can be vanishingly small.

This problem can only be understood by looking through a probabilistic lens. In a deterministic world, if you ask each expert what the most likely outcome will be on each individual part, each one will answer – honestly and accurately – that it's almost a dead certainty that the specifications can be met. Sum up the "most likely" results, and you'll forecast almost certain success. The problem is, with so many parts, you're not always going to get the "most likely"; you're bound to get a few "unlikely" results. And that's all it takes.

Buried in Paper

One technique that is sometimes used when dealing with uncertainty is to play "What If?" – as in:

◆ "What if our sales are really low next year, but everything else is largely the same?"

◆ "What if that new plant takes longer than expected to come on line?"

◆ "What if we get the funding to open that new store, but interest rates go up, and our inventory write-off is higher than usual?"

This approach can help to answer questions regarding specific scenarios, but unless you've got only a few possibilities, it doesn't take long before you're swamped with numbers. Even after you're buried alive under all this printout, you still don't have much of an idea about the *probability* of any of these scenarios occurring, nor do you know what to put into the plan as a target forecast for the future. In short, you have lots of numbers, but it's hard to know what to do with them.

Endless discussions often result about which assumptions are "correct," how likely certain pessimistic scenarios are to occur, and whether it's worth spending time and money to take steps to mitigate against those scenarios.* You don't know which uncertainties are your real value drivers and which ones can safely be treated as "known." The decision-maker is left with a choice: go ahead and make the decision despite the fact that no real insights have been gained, or tell your technical staff to go back and generate more numbers in the hope that the second round of analysis will be more useful than the first. (Albert Einstein defined "insanity" as doing

*The Risk Matrix

In classic risk analysis, a three-dimensional matrix is created for identified risks, plotting magnitude of impact vs. probability of occurrence vs. cost of mitigation. You cannot take sensible action without plotting all three coordinates. Playing "What If" ignores the probability axis, and therefore impedes your ability to make appropriate plans.

the same thing over and over again, and expecting different results.)

High Enough For You?

A third approach to handling uncertainty is to use low, medium, and high estimates for your input parameters to build low, medium, and high cases for the output value of interest (e.g., the NPV of your project). This is trickier than you might expect. Consider Table 3.1.

In this simple case, the parameter of interest is just the sum of the values of A, B and C (like rolling individual assets up to the portfolio level). We've estimated low, medium, and high values for each parameter. How do we determine appropriate low, medium, and high cases for the total? Many companies do what has been done here: the low values are summed to create a low total, the mediums are summed to create a medium total, and likewise for the highs.

But there's a big problem with this. We obviously believe that it is unlikely that A will have a value less than 5, or that B will be less than 10, or that C will be less than 20. However, the probability of *three* unlikely events all occurring at once is much lower than the probability of a single such event (think of the probability of rolling three dice and having them all come up sixes, versus the probability of rolling a six with one die). So the probability of occurrence for the total shown here (35) is extremely low. It is probably so low as to be outside the range worth considering. And as more and more inputs are summed, this probability rapidly plummets even further.

Parameter	Low	Med	High
A	5	10	20
B	10	20	30
C	20	30	50
TOTAL	35?	60?	100?

Table 3.1. Low/Medium/High

The Low-Medium-High Problem – A Statistical Perspective

For those who have some background in statistics, here is a parallel discussion of the Low-Medium-High case that gets into the numbers in a bit more detail.

Let's assume that these are true p_{10}, p_{50}, and p_{90} values, i.e., they represent the 10th, 50th, and 90th percentiles of the total ranges of possible values for each of these parameters. So Parameter A has a 10% chance of being less than 5, a 50/50 chance of being less than 10, and a 10% chance of being greater than 20, and likewise for B and C with respect to the values given for them.

Now – how do we determine appropriate low, medium, and high cases for the total, such that they also represent the true p_{10}, p_{50}, and p_{90} scenarios? If there is only a one-in-ten chance that A has a value less than 5, and a one-in-ten chance that B is less than 10, and a one-in-ten chance that C is less than 20, what are the odds that the total will be less than 35? Certainly not one-in-ten!

As it ends up, the answer depends on the shapes of the probability distributions for each parameter, but with three inputs, the "low" total here is usually something close to the true p_{02} or p_{03} – i.e., there's only about a 2 or 3 percent chance that the total could be less than 35. As more and more inputs are summed, this percentile rapidly plummets.

Likewise, on the high side, there is only about a 2 or 3 percent chance that the total in this case could be greater than 100 (and again, with more inputs, you're into the one-in-a-thousand or one-in-ten-thousand range). We end up with a high-end estimate that would be embarrassing to show to anybody.

On the high side, the same phenomenon occurs: the probability that the total in this case could be greater than 100 is essentially negligible (and again, with more inputs, it gets even worse). We end up with a high-end estimate so unlikely to be realized that we probably wouldn't even want to show it to anybody for fear of losing credibility.

How useful is this from a business perspective? Nobody makes decisions based on scenarios that have impossibly small probabilities of occurrence. (One exception would be the insurance industry, which lives and dies by how well it manages rare, high-impact occurrences. Insurance executives, therefore, have to have a solid understanding of probabilistic methods.) Such scenarios can generally be safely ignored, and that's exactly what happens. Usually, we're interested in a

Adding Numbers That Shouldn't Be Added

Sometimes, we have no choice but to add numbers that theoretically shouldn't be added. For example, the Securities and Exchange Commission requires all oil and gas companies operating in the U.S. to estimate proved reserves for each asset, and then sum these numbers to give the company's total proved reserves. Proved reserves are defined as those hydrocarbons that are "reasonably certain" to be produced, given current plans and prices – i.e., they're our "Low" estimates. We've seen that summing "Low" estimates yields a fairly meaningless number. But if the law requires it, the law requires it.

range that covers about 80% or 90% of the possible outcomes. The 100% confidence range includes too many absurdly unlikely outliers to be of any real use. As such, the results of the Low and High summations in a case like this are equally useless.

This issue of the appropriate range for the output parameter of interest is not a trivial one, nor is it just an academic curiosity. Suppose, for instance, you have five widget plants, each with an uncertainty range regarding the number of widgets it can manufacture in a year, and you are bidding on a contract to become the sole supplier of widgets to Mammoth Corporation for its new product line. How many widgets per year can you safely commit to? You want to capture as much of Mammoth's business as you can (i.e., commit to as much as possible) without taking too high a risk that you'll fail to meet your obligations (the penalties for failure to deliver in such contracts may be severe). How do you arrive at an overall quantity that you are, say, 90% sure you can meet? Simply adding up the p_{10}s for each of your plants will yield a number far too conservative – at the very least you'll be conceding more of the market to your competitors than you should, and you might put yourself out of contention for the contract altogether. You need a good p_{10} estimate of the *total* widget production. We'll look at some appropriate techniques for determining such an estimate in the next chapter.

A common – and equally incorrect – variation on the high-medium- and low-cases is to arbitrarily adjust each key input up and down by 10% (or 20%) and see what happens to the measure of value. The problem with this approach is that there is no rational basis for increasing and decreasing all of the variables by the same percentage. A range of plus or minus 10% on one variable may be reasonable, but it may be very unlikely or even impossible for another variable. This approach can be used as a qualitative check on the computations in a model, but the output is unlikely to be of any real value to the decision maker(s).

So each of the three traditional approaches to handling uncertainty – ignoring it, playing "what if" to examine specific scenarios, and creating high- medium- and low-cases– has problems. We need a more thorough handling of uncertainty if we're really going to understand our business and make optimal strategic decisions.

Points to Ponder

Among the earliest adopters of probabilistic analysis were oil and gas exploration and production companies and companies heavily involved in pharmaceutical research and development.

- Why do you think these two completely unrelated industries were early adopters of probabilistic analysis?
- What other industries and businesses could benefit from probabilistic analysis? Why?

Endnotes

1. The three bullet points and accompanying text are modified from a course instruction manual by Decisioneering Inc., the makers of Crystal Ball® Monte Carlo simulation software. I have changed the words, but the ideas are theirs, and are used with permission.

"He who knows not, and knows not that he knows not, is a fool – shun him.
He who knows not, and knows that he knows not, is a child – teach him.
He who knows, and knows not that he knows, is asleep – wake him.
He who knows, and knows that he knows, is wise – follow him."
– Persian proverb

4

Steps in the Right Direction

We introduce three valuable tools in this chapter: the sensitivity analysis "tornado" chart, the decision tree, and Monte Carlo simulation. Each has its uses, each has its pitfalls, none is sufficient by itself, and all should be used – regularly – to gain insight into an uncertain world.

DEFINITIONS

Dependency:

The terms "dependency" and "correlation" are sometimes used interchangeably. They probably shouldn't be, as statistics texts fairly clearly distinguish between the two concepts. *Dependency* refers to a real-world relationship between two factors. For example, the price of aluminum depends on the quantity of bauxite mined. It depends on other things, too – how much aluminum is recycled, how many car parts are made from aluminum vs. steel or plastic, etc. – but there is a definite dependency between these two items. Likewise, the value of GM's spare parts business depends on the number of new vehicles sold; the higher the sales rate, the higher the expected future demand for spare parts.

Correlation:

A mathematical relationship between two sets of data which indicates the probability that a dependency exists between the parameters underlying the two data sets and the strength of that dependency. (This is not the definition you'll find in a statistics text. Rather than get into linear regressions, I've tried to explain these concepts in terms that non-mathematicians can understand.)

If the examination of a statistically valid sample set of number pairs reveals such a relationship, a correlation is said to exist between these two parameters. As an example, if you were to plot the heights versus the weights of a thousand randomly selected individuals, you would find a strong correlation between the two parameters. The reason for this is the *dependency* that exists between height and weight; taller people usually have more mass – and therefore weigh more – than shorter people. This is the normal state of affairs: a strong correlation between two parameters usually indicates a dependency between those parameters. Knowing the value of one parameter will generally give you an idea about the value of the other (but not always – more on this in Chapter 14).

Note that a correlation need not be a sign of a direct cause-and-effect dependency, like height and weight or bauxite and aluminum. The two parameters may both be dependent on a third parameter. Sales of down jackets may exhibit a correlation with sales of ski resort lift tickets, but there's no direct relationship; rather, both are dependent on the weather. Sales of spiral notebooks and new cars may show a fairly strong correlation, but only because the month in which the new car models come out just happens to approximately coincide with the start of the new school year. Be careful about inferring cause-and-effect relationships from correlations!

Even more importantly, a *lack* of correlation does not necessarily mean that the two parameters are unrelated. A somewhat trivial (but easily understood) example might be the height of a kicked soccer ball vs. the elapsed time since it was kicked. At first, height increases with time, but then the ball turns around and comes back down. Because the equation is parabolic, not linear, a linear regression will show no correlation between height and time in this case. But there's obviously a relationship – a dependency – between the two values.

Distribution Types:

Discrete Distribution:

A probability distribution or histogram in which only certain values within the range are possible. For example, the range of possible values for the roll of a die is from 1 to 6, but only integers are possible. Ditto for the number of flights handled in one day at any given airport gate – you can't have 9.3 flights arrive at gate 33A.

Continuous Distribution:

A probability distribution or histogram in which any value within the range is possible. Examples: the pressure inside a brewery vat, or next year's retail sales of down parkas (granted, it has to be a whole number of cents, but when the units are extremely small relative to the actual value, the distribution is most appropriately modeled as continuous).

Frequency Distribution:

For discrete output distributions, a chart plotting values along the x-axis and the probability of occurrence for each value along the y-axis (see Figure 4.1). For continuous output distributions, the frequency distribution is a histogram in which the x-axis is divided into a large number of "bins" of equal size and the y-axis shows the probability of occurrence of a value within any given bin. When the bin size becomes very small, the distribution approaches a smoothly varying, continuous function.

With a continuous frequency distribution (like Figure 4.2), the y-axis values are completely dependent upon the number of bins used in creating the chart; therefore, *the absolute values along the y-axis are meaningless*. This is because the probability of any specific x-axis value occurring *exactly* is essentially zero. The chart shows the *relative* probability of occurrence for values along the x-axis.

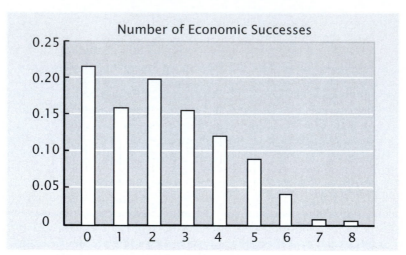

Figure 4.1. Discreet Frequency Distribution

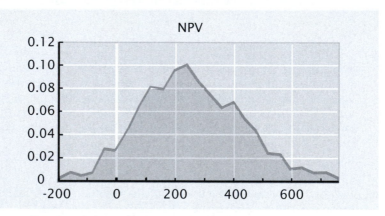

Figure 4.2. Continuous Frequency Distribution

Cumulative Distribution, also called "S-curve" (even though they don't always look like an "S"):

Values are plotted along the x-axis and the probability of occurrence of a value *less than or equal to* the given x-value is plotted along the y-axis. The y-axis, therefore, goes from 0 to 1. Note that the values along the y-axis are meaningful for both the discrete and the continuous cases when it comes to cumulative dis-

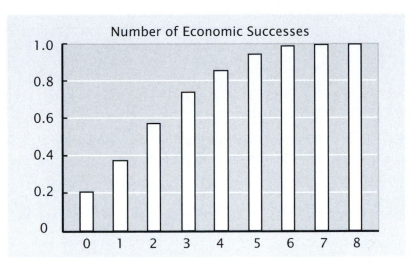

Figure 4.3. Discrete Cumulative Distribution

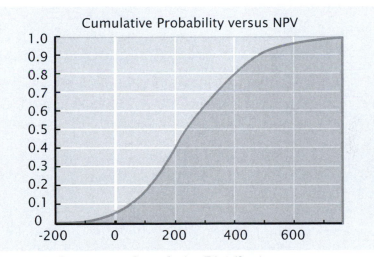

Figure 4.4. Continuous Cumulative Distribution

tributions (Figures 4.3 and 4.4, respectively). (Reverse Cumulative Distributions are sometimes used, too. In this case, the y-axis value represents the probability of occurrence of a value *greater than* or equal to the given x-value.)

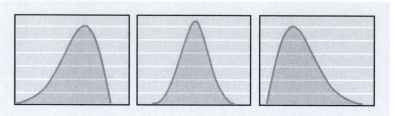

*Figure 4.5. Left-Skewed, Symmetrical, and Right Skewed
Frequency Distributions, Respectively*

Skew:

> A term used to describe distributions that are not symmetrical
> about the mean. In a right-skewed distribution, the extreme val-
> ues on the high side are farther from the mean than are the ex-
> treme values on the low side. In a left-skewed distribution, the
> extreme values on the low side are farther from the mean than
> are the extreme values on the high side (see Figure 4.5).

Tornado Warnings

Many companies have begun to take at least some steps
toward improving the way they deal with uncertainty. They
know they must identify key input parameters – i.e., figure
out which uncertainties have the potential to have the greatest effect on the outcome. This is called a sensitivity analysis,
and the most common tool for this type of analysis is the tornado chart.

When used in a sensitivity analysis, a tornado chart requires at least three values for every input parameter of interest: a low estimate, a medium estimate, and a high estimate. Ideally, these should be estimates of specific statistics
– for example, the p_{10} / p_{50} / p_{90} values (i.e., 10th, 50th, and
90th percentiles of the predicted range of values for that parameter) – but unfortunately, they are often just someone's
subjective idea of low, medium, and high. You then set all parameters to their medium estimates, and calculate the value
of interest (e.g., NPV). This number forms the center line of
the tornado (see Figure 4.6).

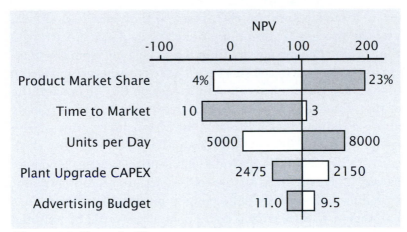

Figure 4.6. Tornado Chart

You then set one parameter to its low value – keeping all others at their medium values – and recalculate. You repeat with that parameter set to its high value, and these two results determine the lengths of the arms of the tornado for that parameter.

For example, in Figure 4.6, this company has built a spreadsheet that takes estimates for a number of input parameters, including the five listed down the left-hand side of Figure 4.6, and calculates the NPV of developing and producing a new product. They have generated low, medium, and high estimates for each of these input parameters, and we'll give them the benefit of the doubt – we'll assume that these are their p_{10}, p_{50}, and p_{90} estimates (as opposed to just a qualitative "low, medium, and high"). Figure 4.6 shows that when all of the input parameters are set to their p_{50} (medium) values, the estimated NPV of the project is about $110 million (the center line of the tornado).

The company believes that there is an 80% chance that their share of the market for the new product will be somewhere between 4% and 23%. When Product Market Share is set to 4% (and all others are kept at their p_{50} values), the NPV falls to about –$25 million; when Product Market Share is set to 23%, the NPV rises to almost $200 million. These figures generate the uppermost arms of the tornado in Figure 4.6.

All parameters are then reset to their medium values, and the process is repeated for each parameter in turn. You then order the parameters from top to bottom, from the longest tornado arms to the shortest. Those parameters at the top of the chart have the greatest influence on the variance of the output; they become your "key uncertainties." In the example above, Product Market Share is the biggest driver of value on the project, but Time to Market and Units/Day are also critical. All three should be considered key uncertainties, and may be worth investigating further to see if the uncertainties might be reduced. The advertising budget, on the other hand, does not appear to have such a big impact. One would be tempted to treat it deterministically for now (i.e., using a single "best estimate").

When constructed correctly, sensitivity analysis tornado charts are a great way to visualize which parameters warrant further attention, and which can safely be ignored for now. Even when thrown together quickly, tornados are a good way to get a rough idea of which uncertainties are *likely* to be important during the analysis.

But tornado charts have their weaknesses, too. One major concern is that tornado charts often take no account of correlations and dependencies between input variables. In the above example, as more money is spent on advertising, the NPV of the project decreases (which makes sense at a superficial level; spend more, and your NPV drops). But increasing one's advertising budget is likely to increase the market share – the biggest driver of value in the model. Tornados usually don't capture this; they are generally created by varying one uncertainty at a time. So when the advertising budget is set to its high value in the tornado, the product market share is at its medium value. This doesn't necessarily make tornados wrong – after all, the market share might remain moderate despite the heavy advertising – but it's definitely something to be aware of. The impact of a variable can change significantly when dependencies are incorporated. Correlations can be included in the analysis (and they sometimes are), but this

makes the assessment and computation processes more difficult. Most tornado charts are made without using correlations.

An even bigger issue is that people often generate the
high and low values for parameters by simply adding and
subtracting some amount (say, 10% or 20%) from the medium
value (which is usually somebody's best guess as to the value
of the parameter). This approach has two serious flaws:

♦ First – as mentioned before – different parameters rarely
  have identical ranges of uncertainty. The price of a volatile commodity is likely to have a much greater uncertainty range than, say, labor rates on a construction site.
  It is inappropriate to model both with a simple +/– 10%.
♦ Second, even within one parameter, uncertainty is rarely
  symmetrical. If all goes well, the weather cooperates, and
  the gods smile on us, we might come in 15% under budget on a major capital project; if everything goes to hell
  in a hand basket, we might end up 200% over budget or
  more. You may have noticed that the tornado in Figure
  4.6 is highly asymmetrical. This is normal. If anyone ever
  shows you a tornado with nice, neat, symmetrical arms
  for all or almost all of the uncertainties, treat it with
  great suspicion.

Sensitivity analysis tornado charts are great, but be aware of
their limitations.

Seeing the Forest for the Trees

So you've created a tornado chart and identified your key
uncertainties. Now what?

One approach is to create a decision tree using the p_{10},
p_{50}, and p_{90} values of the key uncertainties you determined
from your tornado. (Decision trees are usually called this, even
if there is no decision in the tree. Figure 4.7, for example,
contains uncertainties, but no decisions. We'll get into decision trees with actual decisions in later chapters.) Figure 4.7
is just such a tree. It explores every possible combination of

the p_{10}, p_{50}, and p_{90} values for each of the three key uncertainties at the top of our tornado chart in Figure 4.6 (market share, time-to-market, and units/day). Thus, it has twenty-seven (3^3) branches.

Decision trees are created left-to-right, which usually represents the chronological order in which events will occur, uncertainties will be resolved, and decisions will be made. In this case, we will find out how long it takes us to get to market first, then we will discover how many units per day our plant can actually manufacture, and only after we have been producing for a while will we know what our market share is.

At each node of the tree, appropriate probabilities are assigned to the three possible values of that uncertainty.* The probability of each of the twenty-seven end branches is just the product of the probabilities at each node as you move through the tree from left to right.

In order to estimate the Expected Value (EV) of the project, we must calculate the Net Present Value (NPV) for each of the twenty-seven branches and then solve the tree from right to left. For a tree with in which all nodes are uncertainties (like the one in Figure 4.7), the EV is the probability-weighted average of these end values (about $32 million in this case). (When trees have decision nodes, the highest value at each decision node is selected [or the lowest, depending on the purpose of the tree]. With a decision, we get to *choose* what we want.) We can also derive a cumulative probability curve – often called an "S" curve – that displays the range of possible values for this project's NPV, and the probabilities associated with those values (see Figure 4.8).

We can now compare the Expected Value of this project with that of other opportunities we are considering. We can compare the downside risk and the upside potential, and make

---

*Preserving the Mean and Variance

The "0.3" and "0.4" values on the tree in Figure 4.7 are commonly used with p_{10}, p_{50}, and p_{90} inputs because (as has been established in a number of academic papers by R.I. Swanson and others) using these probability weightings best preserves the mean and variance of the original distribution in most cases.

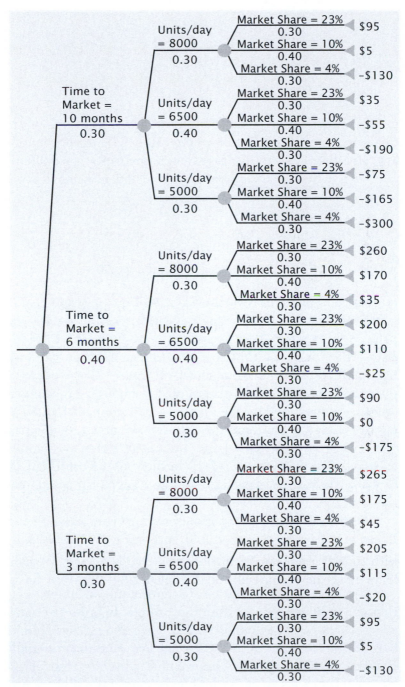

Figure 4.7. Decision Tree

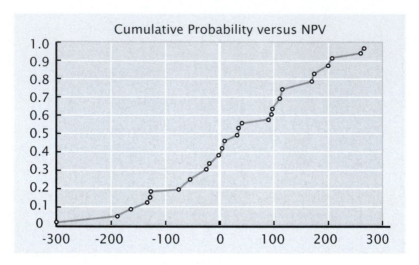

Figure 4.8. "S" Curve Created from Decision Tree

an informed decision regarding which of our projects represents the best opportunity for the company. Had we simply
used a single point "best guess" estimate for each of the inputs – the estimates that comprise the center line value of
$110 million on the tornado chart in Figure 4.6 – we would
never have realized that this project has about a 37% chance
of losing money (and on the upside, a 10% chance of an NPV
greater than $200 million – see Figures 4.8 and 4.9). We also
would have overestimated the amount of value we should
expect this project to add ($110 million vs. $32 million). A
probabilistic analysis yields far more insight than a deterministic one.

Decision trees are very good tools for visualizing all the
likely scenarios that may unfold, assigning probabilities to
them, and estimating the Expected Values of different courses
of action. However, they, too, have some weaknesses.

First, many uncertainties are continuous variables – i.e.,
they can hold any value within their range. In order to create
a tree, certain values (usually the p_{10}, p_{50}, and p_{90}) are chosen
to represent portions of the range (the low, medium, and high
portions, respectively). This approximation is often harmless,
but sometimes it can cause problems, especially if there are

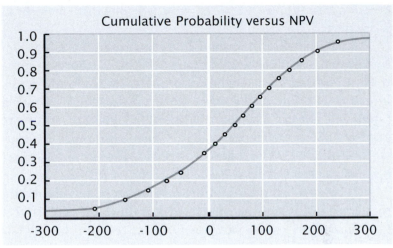

Figure 4.9. Smooth "S" Curve Created with Monte Carlo
         Simulation

natural thresholds in the range that cause step changes in behavior or decisions.

Second, "S" curves derived from decision trees often have artificial "steps" in them. Note the kinks and angles in the curve in Figure 4.8 (for instance, near the point where NPV equals zero). These have no basis in reality; the uncertainties that fed into the NPV calculation are all smoothly varying functions, and we would expect the NPV curve to vary smoothly, too. Unless at least one of your uncertainties has actual step functions in it (i.e., abrupt changes from one value to another) or your value calculation has thresholds or decision points that cause discrete changes at certain levels, your output "S" curve should be relatively smooth. Compare Figure 4.8 with Figure 4.9, which was created with the same input data, but using Monte Carlo simulation* rather than a

*Monte Carlo

"Monte Carlo" refers not only to the simulation process, but also to a specific sampling methodology. "Stochastic" is a more generic term referring to probabilistic simulation, regardless of the sampling method. However, the term, "Monte Carlo simulation" has become widespread in business today, and is the one I have used in this book.

decision tree. Figure 4.9 shows a much smoother, more realistic curve.

This problem is enormously exaggerated if a single uncertainty has a much larger impact on the measure-of-value than all others – i.e., if its arms on the tornado are much larger than those of the other uncertainties. The resulting "steps" (as seen in Figure 4.10) can be misleading – they are artifacts of the tree methodology. I have seen a client incorrectly estimate the probability of losing money on a project because of these "stair steps."

Third, if you have a significant number of key uncertainties, trees can rapidly become impenetrable forests. With five key uncertainties, for example, a typical tree will have 3^5, or 243 branches. This can be unwieldy at times, and certainly ruins the tree's value as a visualization tool.

Having read all this, you might think that I don't trust decision trees, or that I don't like to use them. Nothing could be further from the truth. I use them all the time. When used appropriately –with awareness of their limitations – decision trees are fantastic tools for characterizing and *understanding* the interplay between uncertainties and decisions. This is especially true when they are used in conjunction with Monte Carlo simulation.

Monte Carlo Simulation: "What Ifs" on Steroids

Another excellent tool is Monte Carlo simulation. In a Monte Carlo model, key parameters are input in a different way. Rather than using single, "best estimate" values or discrete high, medium, and low values, each key uncertainty is characterized by giving a range of possible values for that parameter, and a probability distribution associated with that range. For example, the Product Market Share parameter from the tornado chart a couple of pages back looks like Figure 4.11.

This happens to be a lognormal distribution – skewed with a longer tail on the high side. The probability that the Product Market Share will be close to a specific value is pro-

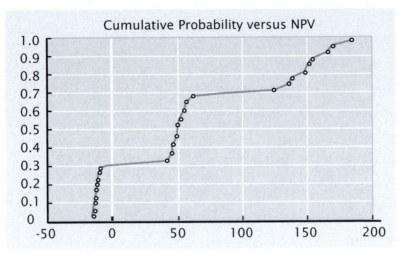

Figure 4.10. "S" Curve Resulting from Decision Tree with One
Dominant Uncertainty

portional to the height of the curve at that point (the relative height of the curve is all that's important here – the actual numbers along the y-axis are fairly meaningless). Thus, values from about 4% up to about 10% – those near the peak of the curve – are believed to be relatively likely; those out on the tails of the distribution – say, down below 2% or above 18% – are possible, but not very likely. Anything lower than 1% or higher than about 32% is almost impossible.

A similar distribution is created for every key uncertainty in the model (they probably won't all be lognormal – there are a number of different types of distributions to choose from). When the Monte Carlo simulation is started, the computer selects a value for each input – honoring the range and probability distribution for each individual input, so you're more likely to get a value near the peak of the curve than out on the tails of the curve – and calculates whatever output metrics you're interested in (NPV in this case, but you might also want to know Year One cash flow, etc.). It gets a value for each output and stores it. Then the simulator goes back through the whole process again, selecting new values for each

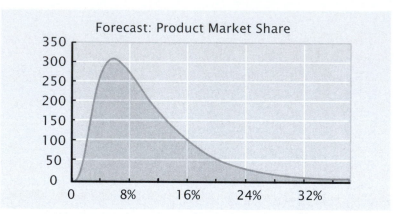

Figure 4.11. Probability Distribution for Product Market Share

input, running through the calculations, getting a new value for each output, and storing them, too.

It repeats the process however many times you like – usually a few hundred at least, and often several thousand – and ultimately ends up with a long list of possible values for each output of interest. The computer then rank orders each list from smallest to largest, calculates statistics based on each list, and displays a histogram of the outputs – i.e., a probability distribution for each output. And that's all there is to it – no magic, just a lot of repetition using certain rules, and subsequent statistical analysis.

This is essentially the "What If" scenario gone wild, but with one huge difference: by choosing the input values at random (albeit while honoring probability distributions) and by performing a statistically significant number of trials, *the outputs become statistically meaningful.* This means you can actually tell something about the probability of, say, achieving an NPV that exceeds a certain threshold, or (on the negative side) the likelihood that you will fail to meet next year's sales growth target, given your current plans. You can also get a much better idea of what to *expect* to achieve from each asset, and therefore, from your portfolio of assets.

This is no small feat. Everyone knows it's important to understand the risks associated with one's plans. However, many people don't seem to grasp that understanding risk means *estimating the probabilities* of various scenarios actually occurring, given your best information today.

For most calculated measures of value (like NPV or ROCE – Return on Capital Employed), there are simply too many contributing components for anyone to have a good gut feel about the range of possible values, let alone the associated probability curves. The best way to estimate these ranges and probabilities is to build a Monte Carlo model to calculate the values, and then estimate probabilities and ranges for the model *inputs* (which are invariably easier to estimate with some degree of reliability). You then run the Monte Carlo simulator and analyze the output distributions, gleaning insights as you do so.

For example, the "S" curve in Figure 4.9 indicates that you have about a thirty-seven percent probability of losing money. Your tornado chart indicates that time-to-market is a significant contributor to the downside, but not to the upside – i.e., taking too long to get to market reduces project value dramatically, but getting to market early doesn't seem to help much. So putting enough resources into project management to keep things on time would probably be a good way to avoid a negative NPV, but accelerating doesn't add much value. Information like this can help you to deploy resources optimally.

At this point, I need to insert a huge caveat. Monte Carlo simulation is, indeed, a wonderful tool, but like any other type of analysis, it's "garbage in/garbage out" – and it's very easy to hide the garbage. In the hands of a Machiavellian type, a Monte Carlo simulator is downright dangerous. He can tweak a bit here and a bit there, choose an optimistic probability distribution on a key parameter or two, and voila: you get the result he wants (or the result he thinks you want). This fear of manipulation is another reason that many managers shy away from stochastic methods. They don't trust what they don't understand.

The answer, however, is not to forego probabilistic analysis. The answer is to climb the learning curve (that's why you bought this book). Then you can make sure the people creating the models and inputting the data don't allow their personal perspectives to bias their objectivity (and make sure *your* personal perspectives don't bias their objectivity, either)

If you're serious about understanding and managing risk and uncertainty in your business, Monte Carlo simulation is an excellent way to go – especially when used in tandem with decision trees. Few tools have the potential to yield so much insight.

Points to Ponder

What do you think the biggest potential pitfalls are when starting to use tools like simulation? How can these potential pitfalls be mitigated?

Keep on Truckin'

A commodities trading firm faced a puzzle while trying to plan its transportation budget for the year. Every unit sent could be transported one of two ways: the firm could pay for Free On Board (FOB) shipping and then truck it to the final destination, or they could pay a straight delivery fee and leave it up to the contractor to decide how to get the commodity there. The firm could (and would) always choose the cheaper of these two alternatives, but they would never know ahead of time which alternative would be cheaper.

So how were they to know how much to budget for transportation costs this year? They had created a forecast for the expected number of units, but they did not know how much they would ultimately end up paying to transport each unit.

To simplify the problem, they broke the possibilities into discrete cases: a high- and low-cost case for each of the three transportation components. They then estimated what "typical" high costs and low costs would be for each component, as well as how likely that specific case would be (i.e., the probability of being in the high-cost situation vs. the low-cost one). The estimates appear in Table 4.1.

In this situation, there are eight possible combinations of costs (2 x 2 x 2). The opinion of the trading firm was that these costs vary independently of each other; just because delivery costs are high, that does not mean that the FOB and/or trucking costs will be high.

So it's simply a matter of laying out the eight possible scenarios, seeing what the transportation decision would be in each case (i.e., which method would be cheaper), and then calculating the probability of that scenario occurring (Table 4.2). The probability of any scenario is just the product of the three probabilities associated with its components – e.g., the probability of the first scenario is 6% because the probabilities of the low FOB cost, the low trucking cost, and the low delivery cost are 30%, 50%, and 40%, respectively, and 30% x 50% x 40% = 6%. (Note that the sum of all the probabilities in the table equals 100%. If the sum of the probabilities associated with your scenarios does not equal 100%, something is seriously wrong).

Now it is a simple matter to calculate the expected transportation cost per unit of commodity: it is the probability-weighted average of the costs chosen under each scenario. $3.00 x 6% + $3.00 x 9% + ... etc. = $4.57.

So our commodities trading firm found that they should budget for a transportation cost of $4.57 per unit. This is the Expected Value (EV) of the transportation cost per unit.

	High Cost ($/unit)	Probability	Low Cost ($/unit)	Probability
FOB	$4.00	70%	$2.00	30%
Trucking	$3.00	50%	$1.00	50%
Delivery	$6.00	60%	$4.00	40%

Table 4.1. Commodity Transportaion Costs per Unit

FOB Cost	Trucking Cost	FOB + Trucking	Delivery Cost	Choice	Probability
$2.00	$1.00	**$3.00**	$4.00	FOB/Truck	6%
$2.00	$1.00	**$3.00**	$6.00	FOB/Truck	9%
$2.00	$3.00	$5.00	**$4.00**	Delivery	6%
$2.00	$3.00	**$5.00**	$6.00	FOB/Truck	9%
$4.00	$1.00	$5.00	**$4.00**	Delivery	14%
$4.00	$1.00	**$5.00**	$6.00	FOB/Truck	21%
$4.00	$3.00	$7.00	**$4.00**	Delivery	14%
$4.00	$3.00	$7.00	**$6.00**	Delivery	21%

Table 4.2. Commodity Transportation Scenarios – Cheaper Alternatives in Bold

In reality, of course, the costs can have any value within the predicted range; they are continuous distributions. It would have been more accurate to model them as such, and then build a simple Monte Carlo simulation model to estimate the average transportation cost per unit. But this approximation was close enough to give the firm a good idea of what their transportation costs for the year would be.

Ironically, never in any of the scenarios do they actually experience a transportation cost of $4.57/unit. This is not unusual; the EV is often a number that you will never realize on any one trial. Think of flipping a coin and winning $1.00 if it comes up heads; the EV = $0.50, but you will always either realize $1.00 or $0.00, never $0.50.

Nor are they even likely to experience an *average* transportation cost for the year of exactly $4.57/unit. If they ship a large number of units the average will probably be very close to that figure (assuming that their input assumptions were valid), so it is still an excellent estimate to use when planning the budget. But the probability of hitting it exactly is slim, indeed.

"If a man will begin in certainties he shall end in doubts; but if he will be content to begin in doubts he shall end in certainties."
– Sir Francis Bacon

"Certainty is learning's enemy...."
– John H. Lienhard

5

Improving the Odds of Success

In this chapter, we define risk-neutrality and show why it is a key to corporate success. We also touch on the human tendency toward risk aversion (which is explored more fully in Chapter 6). We show why expecting each individual project to succeed wastes one of the greatest advantages a company has: the ability to absorb losses and share rewards.

How Fear of CLMs Causes CEs to be Less Than EVs, Thereby Reducing NPVs*

"We want bold risk-takers to lead our company."

Does this sound familiar? A senior vice-president at a former employer of mine made this statement at an employee town hall meeting, and when I've repeated it to other people, many claim to have heard similar things from their senior managers. It's not unusual for management to come out with a proclamation like this at one time or another. It's designed to inspire the troops and make them feel empowered to live life on the edge.

Now how about this one: "Everyone will be held absolutely accountable for the results from his or her business unit." Yes, there's a familiar and righteous ring to this statement, too: "No excuses! We all take responsibility for what we do!"

The problem is, in an uncertain world, these two sentiments are incompatible. If my bonus, promotion, continued employment, etc. depend on my delivering the goods, there is no way I'm going to risk failure by embarking on a high-potential-but-significant-probability-of-failure project, regardless of how high the statistical mean, or EV, might be. I'm going to play it safe, as will most people.

Michael Allen describes this situation in *Business Portfolio Management* (Allen p. 89-91). A vice-president of one of Allen's clients very eloquently lays out the conundrum of business managers who are "judged as if risk did not exist, and if we even mention it, we are accused of making excuses." They are further expected to "sign in blood that 'This is what I can deliver.'" (Ironically, many senior executives have no problem acknowledging uncertainty when it comes to the investment commitments *they* have made. If revenue is down one year, project budgets are routinely slashed across the board, regardless of what had been previously promised to the project managers (Allen p. 95)).

---

*How fear of Career-Limiting Moves causes Certain Equivalents to be less than Expected Values, thereby reducing Net Present Values

How, then, is a company like this supposed to develop a corporate strategy that deals intelligently with the uncertainties that abound in their world? How are these energetic, talented men and women supposed to take reasonable risks in order to pursue projects and plans that will add value to the company? Quite simply, they won't.

Remaining Neutral

The result is under-performance at the corporate level. Companies that shy away from big projects with high expected values (but relatively low probabilities of success) in favor of safer projects with lower expected values are leaving money on the table (unless the failure of the big project could break the company – more on that later).

Conversely, those that overcome the human tendency toward risk aversion (and reward their managers for doing the same) will, on average, outperform those that do not. Assuming you're in business for the long haul, i.e., you'll be evaluating and embarking on numerous projects for years to come, the best approach is one of risk neutrality.

Risk neutrality, as the name implies, means judging each opportunity based solely on its Expected Value, without additional regard to its probability of success (the EV calculation *already incorporates* probability of success). For example, suppose Project A has a sure NPV of $4 million. Project B is not so certain – it has a success-case NPV of $25 million, a failure-case NPV of –$2 million, and a probability of success of 28%. Despite the uncertainty, Project B should be favored (since $25 million x 28% – $2 million x 72% = $5.56 million, which is larger than $4 million). Companies that consistently choose their Project Bs will out-perform those that choose their Project As in the long run. (This whole discussion assumes that your company is not opportunity-limited – i.e., that you have a greater number of attractive opportunities than you can comfortably fund, and are choosing between them. If this isn't the case – if you have more funds available than you have attractive opportunities to invest in – then you should simply fund every value-adding opportunity you have and/or return funds to your investors in the form of dividends or stock repurchases.)

However, there's a catch to this: you have to be able to afford to lose. More than likely, if you embark on Project B, you're going to lose $2 million. If that's going to break the company or put it into dire financial stress, you obviously should not consider Project B.

In fact, you have to be able to afford to lose numerous times. Statistics will tell you that if you launch eight independent projects, each exactly like Project B, you'll have about a 93% chance of making money – but even that's no guarantee. There is still a 7% chance that at the end of your eight Project Bs, you will have lost $16 million. Just as it is possible (not probable, but possible) to play black all night long in roulette and lose every time, so, too, do the gods of statistics sometimes play cruel games with businesses embarking on risky ventures. But statistics will also tell you that after eight Project Bs, you have a 70% chance of coming out ahead of someone who embarked on eight Project As (and with forty such projects, you could be 83% sure of superior performance).

So how risk-neutral you can afford to be is related to how much capital you have to play with. This is true on a personal level, as well as in business. Offer the following game to people: you flip a coin. If it's heads, you give them $1; if it's tails, they get nothing. It costs 40 cents to play, and you're only allowed to play once. I guarantee almost everybody will want to play.

Now let's raise the stakes by a few orders of magnitude: if it's heads, you give them $1000, but the game now costs $400 to play. Far fewer people will want to participate. Raise the reward to $1 million and the cost to $400,000, and only the wealthiest will be able to play (and many of them won't want to).

What's going on here? In the million-dollar game, it's simple – most people just don't have the money to play even if they want to. But in the thousand-dollar game, many people

Monkey Business

The human tendency toward risk aversion might be heredi-tary – and I'm not talking about getting it from your father or mother. Keith Chen, of the Yale School of Management, and his colleagues performed studies of behavior in capuchin monkeys that yielded some interesting results.[1]

First, the subjects were introduced to small metal disks. The monkeys quickly learned that foolish humans were willing to trade delicious pieces of food for these useless objects, and the world's first Simian cash economy was born. Prices for apple slices, grapes, etc. were soon established.

But then prices were changed. Twice as much apple was of-fered for a single coin, effectively cutting the price in half, while each monkey's allotment of coins dropped from twelve to nine. Demand for apples increased almost exactly in line with what eco-nomic theory would predict (within 1%). So our furry little cousins know a bargain when they see one.

Then the experimenters set up a series of trading regimes. In each regime, the monkeys had to choose between two human "salesmen."

In the first regime, Salesman A offered one apple slice for a disk while Salesman B offered two. But half the time, Salesman B would only hand over one slice after the deal had been completed. The monkeys may not have liked being tricked, but they still figured out that, overall, Salesman B offered the better deal. They gave him most of their business.

In the second regime, Salesman B behaved as before, and Salesman A again offered only one slice, but half the time Sales-man A would turn over a bonus slice after the transaction was com-pleted. Despite the fact that, on average, both salesmen yielded the same number of apple slices, the monkeys quickly came to pre-fer Salesman A. As any good salesman knows, a customer who thinks he's getting something extra is a happy customer; one who feels he's been cheated – rightly or wrongly – will not be back.

In the third regime, Salesman A never gave any freebies, and Salesman B always offered two apple slices, but then only turned over one. The monkeys' preference for Salesman A was even stron-ger than it was during the second regime – despite the fact that the actual yield from both salesmen was again identical.

So it is entirely possible that the human tendency to avoid risk or loss – even perceived risk or loss – is more deeply embedded in our genes than we might have thought. The monkeys showed the ability to make rational assessments of value early in the experiment, but their later behavior was – from a strict economic well-being standpoint – certainly irrational. Humans are much the same.

could play, and the odds are in their favor; the EV of the coin flip is worth more than the cost of the game ($1000 x 50% probability of winning + $0 x 50% probability of losing = $500 > $400). Yet many people who could easily afford to play the game will refuse. To them, the value of the coin toss is less than the value of a sure-fire $400.

Suppose we turn the game around. Instead of charging 40 cents to play the $1 game, we *give* the would-be participant the right to play. But then we ask how much she would be willing to accept to sell that right to someone else. Most people would accept something awfully close to 50 cents – the point at which the EV of the offered price ($0.50) is identical to the EV of the game. But they wouldn't accept significantly less. Offer them, say, $0.45, and they'll probably take the coin flip instead. At this point, most people are risk neutral. Whether they realize it or not, they are multiplying the value of each alternative by its respective probability of occurrence, and basing their decision on these probability-weighted averages (the EVs) without further consideration of the probability of winning or losing.

When the reward goes up to $1000, however, you would get a variety of responses to the "How much would you accept to sell the right to play?" question. Certainly, if you offered $1, nobody would sell; if you offered $550, almost everybody would (there are a few risk seekers out there, but not as many as those who are risk-averse. Risk seekers, like the risk-averse, generate sub-optimal results). Most people would accept something less than $500 – maybe $400, maybe $450. It would vary from person to person. But for every individual, there exists some value – some percentage of the EV of the game – that she would be willing to accept in exchange for the right to play the game.

This amount is called the Certain Equivalent (CE). Certain Equivalents tend to decrease (on a percentage basis) as the amount in question increases. Thus, the CE is 100% when the EV of the game is $0.50, something less than 100% when the EV is \$500, and something even less when the EV is \$500,000.

This is risk aversion, and it is a normal human reaction when faced with potential gains. There are various theories about why it exists, some of which are rooted in ancient man's struggle for survival on the plains of the Serengeti. When you're talking about food, a small amount for sure is worth more than a large amount that you might or might not actually get.

Whatever the source, though, risk aversion is a problem in business. Provided a company has the financial staying power to attempt many projects, the road to optimal performance is to evaluate projects in a risk-neutral manner. Failure to do so – using a utility function, for example, to incorporate one's risk aversion – creates a risk premium, a gap between the value realized using the utility function and the risk-neutral expected value (Skinner, page 236). To maximize the value of your *portfolio* of projects, your Certain Equivalent *at the project level* should be 100% (i.e., your decisions should be risk-neutral).

However, there are two caveats to this rule. First, if failure on an individual project *could* spell disaster for the company, you obviously shouldn't take the risk; it makes more sense to pursue an alternative project with a higher probability of success, even if it has a lower EV. Better still, see if you can find a partner to join you on the high-risk venture, such that the level of exposure for each individual company is acceptable. Many industries use joint ventures to accomplish just this type of risk reduction.

Unfortunately, most managers plunge into joint ventures (or simply walk away from opportunities) at levels of exposure that, while uncomfortable, don't really threaten the continuing viability of the firm. Managers often base their risk tolerance on their own project's budget, not the company's budget (Allen p. 86). This is a huge mistake.

Recall the coin flip game a few paragraphs back. Let's say that heads wins \$10,000, tails wins \$0, and it costs \$4000 to play. Most people would turn down a single chance to play this game. Despite the positive Expected Value, their Certain Equivalents would probably be less than $4000.

Now suppose this game is offered not only to you, but to nine of your close friends, too. Individually, most of you would probably turn down the opportunity to play this game once. But what if you are allowed to discuss, collude, make deals with each other, etc. – in other words, you're allowed to act as a team (or a company). Now what would your decision be?

You should all play the game and share the net proceeds. There is about a 62% chance that you'll come out ahead, plus another 21% chance that you'll break even. This leaves only about a 17% chance you'll lose money – and even then, the probability that each of you will lose more than $1000 is only about 6% (the probability that you will each win more than $1000 is about 38%). At the team level (or portfolio level), the probability of loss is acceptable, even if the risk seems daunting at the individual player level (or project level). If you and your friends make your decisions based on the collective risk/ return probabilities, you are highly likely to do better than another group of people who make decisions based on each individual player's risk tolerance.

The same holds true in business. Paying a premium to eliminate risk at the project level – rather than at the company portfolio level – leads to under-performance overall. However, it is a predictable result if the company's culture and reward mechanisms create an expectation of success (and/ or punishment for failure) on every project. If my bonus and career prospects hinge on having a successful project, I will avoid significant risk – even reasonable risks that result in a higher Expected Value for the company.

The second exception to the risk-neutral rule surfaces when you don't have the opportunity and/or the capital to participate in a statistically valid number of projects. This is part of the reason why people will take a sure-fire $4000 over a coin flip that might land them $10,000 – we're only offering them *one* chance to play. Offer them ten chances to play, and they're in the same situation as you were when you teamed up with your friends. Far more people will accept the opportunity to play.

If the chance of success on any one project is fairly low (as is the case when funding high-tech start-up companies or developing new drugs), it may take a very large number of projects to achieve statistical validity. When you're playing long shots, you need to be able to stay in the game for a long time. If you don't – if you're taking a flier on one or two low-probability ventures – your Certain Equivalent will once again be lower than the EV of the uncertain project.

In business, though, an individual project rarely spells doom for the company if it fails, and new opportunities usually appear on the horizon all the time. A pharmaceutical company doesn't get one chance to develop a drug; rather, it has many different drugs in the pipeline. Most fail and end up costing the company money – but some of the ones that do succeed pay off extremely well. In this situation, the decision to proceed with the testing of drug A rather than drug B should be based solely on the EVs of the two projects, regardless of which one has the higher probability of success. In the long run, you'll make more money.

Nevertheless, I know of several large companies – and we're talking about annual capital budgets well into the billions of dollars – that do not follow a policy of risk neutrality (and I'm sure there are many more of which I am not aware). They superimpose a hurdle rate for probability of success on the valuation of projects – e.g., any project with a probability of success less than, say, 25% is rejected, regardless of how large the potential payoff might be or how low the initial capital investment might be. (Granted, the project is not usually rejected outright. Rather, the project team is told to gather more information in an attempt to reduce the uncertainty to the point where either the probability of success rises above the threshold or – in the event of discouraging data – the EV drops to where the project can be rejected with confidence. Without proper analysis beforehand, however, this is often a waste of company funds. This subject will be discussed in greater detail in Chapter 12, which deals with the Value of Information).

Policies like these are often implemented because of the "no excuses" mantra. If funding a string of failures is a career-limiting move (known as a "CLM" in some firms), I want to be pretty darn sure that I won't go too long without at least one success. Thus, I implement a chance-of-success hurdle, even though in the long run, the company will make less money.

Risk aversion like this also comes into play when a company does a poor job of assessing uncertainty on high-risk projects. One energy client looked back over its record of probability-of-success (sometimes abbreviated as "$p(s)$") predictions. It categorized all exploration projects according to their predicted $p(s)$ – putting all those that were assessed to be between 10% and 20% into one group, those that were assessed to be between 20% and 30% into another, etc. Then they graphed what the *actual* success rate was for the projects in each group.

If all assessments had been perfect, one would find that within the 10% – 20% group, between 10% and 20% would actually have succeeded. Likewise, the 20% – 30% group would show a success rate of between 20% and 30%, and so on. What the client found, however, was quite different. The assessments for projects of moderate risk ($p(s) > 20\%$) were, indeed, fairly reliable. But the success rate for the riskier projects was far worse than predicted: well below 10% for the 10% – 20% group, and almost 0% for the projects with a predicted $p(s)$ of less than 10%.

This was a great piece of self-analysis, and the company should be commended for it. But their solution to the problem was less praiseworthy: they implemented a minimum probability-of-success threshold for all future projects. Rather than use what they learned to improve their assessment skills, they essentially gave up on all high-risk exploration projects, thereby eliminating a number of perfectly good opportunities from consideration. It would have been far more productive to train the technical staff to overcome their bias – in this case, over-optimism – on high-risk opportunities, and then maintain a risk-neutral approach when deciding between projects. The fault, dear Brutus, is not in our projects, but in ourselves, that we are unsuccessful.

In summary, risk neutrality at the project level leads to optimal returns at the portfolio level. But you cannot be risk neutral if you don't even know what the EV of a project is, and you cannot know what that is if you haven't done a probabilistic evaluation. Getting a handle on the uncertainties that contribute to the probability of success for each opportunity is simply critical to the overall performance of any company. Those decision makers who take a rigorous approach to quantifying and understanding the uncertainties surrounding their business opportunities – and aren't afraid to take reasonable risks in the face of those uncertainties – are creating a competitive advantage for their shareholders.

Points to Ponder

Goldman Sachs has been an exceedingly profitable investment bank, the envy of its peers. From 2001-2005, the firm's compound annual growth rate in revenue was 11.9%.[2] In the first quarter of 2006, return on equity was almost 40%.

Most of this revenue has come from trading. Yet, from 2002-2005 inclusive, Goldman Sachs had far more negative trading days (i.e. days on which the firm lost money trading) than did any of its competitors (166 for Goldman Sachs vs. 80 for Morgan Stanley, 42 for Merrill Lynch, and 41 each for Bear Stearns and Lehman Brothers).

Is this what you would expect? Why or why not?

Endnotes

1. *The Economist*, June 25th, 2005, pp. 80-81.
2. *The Economist*, April 27th, 2006.

"If you can keep your head when those about you are losing theirs, you obviously don't understand the situation."
– Hal Roach

6

It's All in Your Head

Humans have struggled with uncertainty for millennia. There are good reasons why this has been such a struggle. In this chapter we briefly investigate several dimensions of human weakness when it comes to dealing with uncertain situations. We look at how framing a problem differently can cause a banker to become a gambler, why it is so hard to kill bad projects, why we should listen to our gut (but not be ruled by it), and much more.

How difficult is it to manage risk and uncertainty? Determining expected values, choosing the appropriate metric, weighing competing opportunities with varying probabilities of success – these are activities that can tax even the brightest and most flexible of managerial minds. And they aren't optional. They have to be done. Whether you handle them explicitly, using the language and concepts promoted in this book, or you handle them implicitly by asking lots of questions, staring thoughtfully out the window, and ultimately following your hunches, business leaders must constantly consider and reconsider the potential risks, rewards, and likelihoods of success of all of the alternative courses of action available. In fact, these issues are a good part of why managing a business can be so difficult.

If you have found yourself occasionally struggling with problems such as these, take heart – you're not alone. Even when the numbers are presented in an honest, straightforward way (and they very often aren't) they can cause confusion in the human mind.

Research in recent decades (much of it by Daniel Kahneman and Amos Tversky) has shown that human beings are remarkably poor at estimating probabilities, and that we are equally poor at reacting rationally to probabilities that are given to us. This has been a bombshell in economic theory, virtually destroying the notion of rational markets (Kahneman was awarded a share of the Nobel Prize for Economics in 2002 for his work; Tversky, unfortunately, had died by that time). It should also call into question the notion (held by many business leaders) that following one's intuition is the best way to make major decisions in an uncertain environment. Some individuals do seem to have an above-average ability to assess uncertain data logically and consistently, but it is dangerous to assume that you're one of the elite few, even if you have an impressive track record of business successes. And even if you are indeed one of the gifted, it's important to understand the weaknesses that are common to most human beings when dealing with uncertain events and probabilities. Most of your employees will fall into this category.

This chapter contains scenarios that illustrate several aspects of illogical, contradictory human behavior in the face of uncertainty. Some of the examples are taken directly from the work of Kahneman and Tversky, Richard Thaler, and others; all have underlying concepts with origins in the pioneering experiments of these men.

It's All Relative – But Should it Be?

You are buying a $125 jacket and a $15 calculator. The store salesman tells you that another branch of the same store has the calculator on sale for $10. This other store is across town, twenty minutes away. Question: would you drive across town to buy these items? About 68% of those surveyed said yes, they would (Kahneman and Tversky pages 11-12). When the prices were reversed, however (the calculator now costs $125, and the jacket, $15) and the same $5 discount is offered on the calculator, only 29% of respondents said they would make the drive across town. It simply wasn't worth it to drive across town to save $5 on a $125 calculator.

But wait – either it's worth $5 to drive across town, or it's not. The *absolute* amount you save is what should be significant here, not the amount *relative* to what you're spending. It is blatantly inconsistent to decide to make the trip for the cheaper calculator, but not for the more expensive one.

Even worse, when the jacket is included, the total amount being spent is exactly the same in both cases! The situation is actually identical in the two surveys: in both cases, you have to choose between buying a jacket and a calculator here for $140, or driving across town and getting them for $135. Yet more than twice as many people were willing to make the trip if the discount was offered on a cheap item rather than an expensive one.

Welcome to the human mind, where logic and consistency don't necessarily rule.

Reference Frames 1: The Plague

A disease is spreading in your city, and you are responsible for deciding what to do about it. It has been estimated that 600 people will die from this disease if nothing is done. Doctors tell you that there are two alternative programs for attacking the problem (Kahneman and Tversky pages 4-5):

- ◆ Under Program A, 200 people will definitely be saved.
- ◆ Under Program B, there is a 33% chance that 600 people will be saved, and a 67% chance that no one will be saved.

Which program would you choose?

When Kahneman and Tversky presented people with this situation, 72% of the subjects chose Program A, and only 28% chose Program B.

But wait – two new programs arise:

- ◆ Under Program C, 400 people will definitely die.
- ◆ Under Program D, there is a 33% chance that no one will die, and a 67% chance that 600 people will die.

Of these two new alternatives, which would you choose?

When presented with this choice, 78% of the subjects chose Program D, and only 22% chose Program C.

By now, you should have noticed something funny. Programs A and C are identical, and so are Programs B and D. In both A and C, 200 people live and 400 die; in both B and D, you have a 33% chance of saving all 600 people, and a 67% chance of losing all of them. Yet people preferred Program A to Program B, and Program D to Program C! How is this possible? Are people really that unreliable and inconsistent?

The short answer is yes, we are.

For many years, conventional wisdom held that most people are risk-averse. Given the choice between a sure-fire $1000 and a 50% chance of getting $2000, most people will opt for the former. In fact, given the choice between a sure-fire $1000 and a 50% chance of getting $2500, most people will opt for the former.

Kahneman and Tversky discovered that when people are looking at gains, they are indeed risk-averse. But when people are looking at losses, it's a different story. The same accountant in the button-down shirt who would rather earn a steady 3.5% on his money than risk it in the stock market will, if given the choice between a sure-fire loss of $1000 or a 50% chance of losing $2000 (or even $2500), will usually opt for the latter. When it comes to potential losses, the banker becomes the gambler (and every casino in Las Vegas knows it). This is the "double-or-nothing" syndrome. We're not risk averse; we're *loss* averse, and we'll go to absurd lengths to avoid a loss – any loss.

It all comes down to how the problem is framed. When we see the Plague scenario in terms of how many lives we'll save, we play it safe and go for the sure-fire 200. When the problem is worded in terms of numbers of deaths, we are suddenly ready to roll the dice, and see if we can't prevent anybody from dying.

Reference Frames 2: Projects and Portfolios

This tendency to play it safe on the upside and risk it all on the downside spills over into the financial world, too. Consider the following pairs of choices (Kahneman and Tversky page 6):

Choice 1:

♦ Project A results in a sure-fire gain of $240.
♦ Project B has a 25% chance of gaining $1000, and a 75% chance of just breaking even.

Most people (84%) chose Project A, even though the Expected Value of Project B ($250) is greater. Now consider choice 2:

♦ Project C results in a sure-fire loss of $750.
♦ Project D has a 25% chance of breaking even, and a 75% chance of losing $1000.

Eighty-seven percent chose Project D, even though the EVs of the two choices are identical (–$750). No big surprises yet.

Projects A and D	Projects B and C
25% chance of +$240	25% chance of +$250
75% chance of -$760	75% chance of -$750
Expected Value = -$510	Expected Value = -$500

Table 6.1. Comparison of Portfolios

But look at what happens if you consider these two choices together. The most popular portfolio – Projects A and D – has a 25% chance of gaining $240, and a 75% chance of losing $760, for an EV of –$510. The least popular portfolio – Projects B and C – has a 25% chance of gaining $250, and a 75% chance losing $750, for an EV of –$500 (see Table 6.1).

What's so amazing about this is not that the EV for B+C is higher – that's to be expected, given that the EV of each of its components is greater than or equal to that of the alternatives. What should give one pause is that B+C is a *less risky* portfolio than is A+D. The upside potential is higher, and the maximum possible loss is smaller. It is definitely the portfolio of choice for anybody who is risk-averse, risk-neutral, or even risk-seeking. Yet when people select the elements of their portfolios one at a time, they often end up with characteristics – lower expected value and higher value at risk – exactly opposite to what they want.

The implication for executives and managers in business is huge. Subconsciously, we often create portfolios that are ill-suited to accomplishing our objectives. We shy away from high-potential long-shot projects that, if they work, could be company-makers. And when we find ourselves mired in a bad project that is losing money hand over fist, as long as there is some chance – however slim – of turning things around so that we don't end up taking a loss, we'll hang in there and fight, throwing good money after bad. Admitting that we've made a mistake and cutting our losses is often the hardest thing to do in business.

And none of this takes into account the effect that sunk costs has on people. We all know that how much we've spent on a project to date should have no effect at all on our decisions from this point forward, but we've all also seen how difficult it is to keep that in mind when you've sunk millions into a project that is spiraling downhill fast. Sunk costs add yet another weight on the psychological scale that tips toward continuing with a bad project, rather than getting out and cutting our losses.

These are examples of why it is so important to understand not only the numbers, but also the people. We need to perform our analyses, but then we also need to think carefully about how we display our results. If you present the same numbers in two different ways, people will draw different conclusions (and make different decisions).

Losses vs. Costs

Kahneman and Tversky found another reason why we're so reluctant to write off bad projects as losses: people dislike losses far more than they dislike costs. Both involve an outflow of money, of course, but psychologically, a loss is far more painful than a cost of equal magnitude.

An example will help. Consider the following game:

♦ 10% chance of winning $95
♦ 90% chance of losing $5.

A number of people said they would play (Kahneman and Tversky page 15). Given the following, slightly different game:

♦ 10% chance of winning $100
♦ 90% chance of winning nothing
♦ a cost of $5 to play the game,

the percentage of people who said they would play went up by 30%. But it's the same game. In both cases, you have a 10% chance of coming out $95 ahead, and a 90% chance of coming out $5 down. The only difference is that in the first game, the $5 is viewed as a loss; in the second, it's a cost. People don't like costs much, but they hate losses with a passion.

This bolsters a typical project manager's refusal to write off a bad project – and even worse, his or her tendency to pour additional money into such a project in an effort to turn it around. As long as the project is alive, the funds we've spent (and continue to spend) are costs; as soon as we write the project off, the negative balance becomes a loss. And people are loss-averse.

Standing on the Fulcrum

Consider another game, one with two players. Player 1 is promised $10, and is told that she may split this amount with player 2 in any proportion she likes, i.e., she may offer player 2 anywhere from $0 to the whole $10. If player 2 rejects the offer, neither player receives any money at all. There is no negotiation – it's a one-time offer, followed by acceptance or rejection.

If everyone acted rationally, player 2 would always accept the offer, no matter how paltry. After all, any amount is better than nothing, which is what he receives if he rejects the offer. Not too surprisingly, however, it doesn't always work that way. If the split is seen to be too unfair, many people turn it down, forfeiting their own gain in order to punish the greed of the other player.

Alan Sanfey of the University of Arizona monitored people's brain activity as they played this game.[1] What he found was competing activity in two areas of the brain: an area of the prefrontal cortex (which deals with logical reasoning and goal orientation), and the anterior insula, a more "primitive" part of our brains that deals with negative emotions like anger and indignation. The more unfair the amount offered, the higher the activity in the latter area. We become angry enough to cut off our nose to spite the other player's face. Emotion overwhelms logic.

This must be a bad thing, right? Obviously, it is best to keep emotion out of decision-making altogether.

Well, maybe not. Neurologist Antonio Damasio studied patients who suffered damage to the part of the prefrontal cortex that processes emotions. Tests showed that these patients suffered no damage to their IQ, memory, language, etc., but when showed intense images of burning buildings and injured people, they felt nothing. They had no emotional response.

They also could not make decisions. Faced with even a minor problem at work or in their personal lives, they'd spend the better part of a day just considering how best to approach the issue. They would examine every possible option, every permutation of possibilities, and never get around to actually achieving anything. With the rational part of their cortexes unchecked by any feelings (or sense of urgency), these people suffered from "analysis paralysis" to the nth degree. Even when the flaw in their approach was pointed out to them, they still couldn't change their behavior.

So decision-making depends on emotion. This isn't really news – organizational behaviorists have known for years that people make most decisions based on emotion. They may collect and examine data, but when it comes time to choose one option or another, most people do what they *feel* is best.

Effective decision making in business, however, requires maintaining an appropriate balance in the interplay between logic and emotion that goes on in our brains. The more primitive part of our brains – what Gardiner Morse calls our "dog brain" – simply cannot comprehend the complex business issues executives have to deal with all the time. We need to keep the cortex involved to make rational sense it all. But if we ignore our feelings and hunches, we forego the power of our subconscious to steer us in the right direction and to help us reach a conclusion. We need to listen to the dog, too.

No Doubt

Another psychological foible of human beings is our tendency to undervalue events with a probability greater than zero and less than one (i.e., anything that isn't certain to turn out one way or another, Kahneman and Tversky pages 7-8). People will pay far more to bring the probability of success on a project from 90% to 100% than they will to raise it from 60% to 75% – even though the latter is obviously worth more. On the negative side – that is, when looking at potential losses

– it's the absolute value that tends to be underestimated. Thus, in the earlier example, the 75% probability of losing $1000 is perceived as having a smaller negative value than a sure-fire loss of $750. We just don't give uncertain events enough weight.

There is one exception to this rule, though: rare, high-impact events. Events – both positive and negative – with a very low probability of occurrence but a large effect if they do occur tend to loom larger than they should in most people's minds. Thus, we buy lottery tickets, even though we have a greater chance of guessing a total stranger's telephone number than we do of winning.* We also buy insurance against all kinds of disasters, both business and personal, even though the odds against them happening are astronomical. We would probably be better off financially by simply taking the risk, and stashing in an investment account the money we normally would spend on premiums. But we just can't bring ourselves to take that risk. What if we turn out to be that one-in-a-million?

Pain and Pleasure: Two Sides of a Loaded Coin

Kahneman and Tversky also found that the pain from a loss is greater than the pleasure from a gain of equal size. This probably doesn't surprise many people. After all, the delight of finding $20 lying in the street is fleeting. The discovery that you've somehow lost $20 on your way to work is infuriating, and can put you into a foul mood for the entire day.

Likewise, if we invest in two projects – one that generates a handsome return for the company and one that loses almost the same amount, resulting in a combined rate of return that is acceptable, but not spectacular – we're not happy. Even if these projects are fairly risky and the probability curves for NPV were known to be broad, even if the return on

---

*In fairness, most people buy lottery tickets for the excitement of the chase, not because they seriously expect to win. But very few people really understand how miniscule their chances are, and how big a waste of money lottery tickets are.

each project falls well within the $p_{10} - p_{90}$ range of expected results, most people will find themselves far more upset about the bad project than they will be pleased about the winner. This makes objective management a challenge.

So losses are more painful than gains are pleasurable. The logical corollary to this, however, is not so obvious: volatility hurts. People who invest in high-potential, volatile stocks and then check on the price twice daily will make themselves miserable (or at the very least, overly anxious), even if the stock goes up in the long run (Taleb pages 56-59). Why? Because the joy they get when they see that it went up $3/share from Monday to Tuesday is nothing compared to the agony they feel when it drops $2.90 by Wednesday. Never mind that by the end of the week, the stock is higher than it was the week before – the roller-coaster ride to get there shreds most people's nerves. In *Fooled by Randomness* (which ought to be required reading to become a business manager), Nassim Nicholas Taleb points out that if these people would just check on their investments less frequently, they'd be happier.

Maybe ignorance really is bliss.

Mine's Better Than Yours

Richard Thaler developed the concept of the Endowment Effect to explain people's tendency to value something they own more highly than an identical object (or asset) that they don't own (Kahneman and Tversky pages 273-276).[2] People will consistently demand a higher price to sell something (or do something) than they are willing to pay when buying an identical asset (or purchasing an identical service). Thus, a man who mows his own lawn refuses to pay the neighbor's son $8 to mow it for him, but also wouldn't mow his neighbor's identical lawn for less than $20. This is logically inconsistent, but common nevertheless.

When you're selling your vase collection on eBay, this bias is fairly harmless. However, if you're buying, selling, and trading your company's assets, this kind of bias can cause you to walk away from deals you ought to be making. When selling an asset, it can be useful to pretend that you're the buyer, not the seller, and try to estimate how much you'd be willing to pay for it (as opposed to how much you'd be willing to accept for it). You might be surprised at how different your estimate is. Ditto when buying an asset – try to put yourself into the seller's shoes.

The Tip of the Iceberg

I have presented a sampler of some of the most important examples of human weakness when it comes to dealing with probabilities, uncertainties, and valuations. There are many others, including (for example) the tendency for people to seek out information that reaffirms their beliefs, and to downplay, ignore, and/or fail to see the significance of information that contradicts those beliefs.[3] If you're interested in delving deeper into subjects like these, the book by Kahneman and Tversky (in the bibliography) contains a large number of papers (by themselves and others) that illustrate many more such psychological quirks. It is very enlightening and amusing reading.

I'd like to add a word of warning. It's easy to brush all of this off with, "Maybe other people are this stupid, but I'm not. I weigh the pros and cons, and I make solid, rational decisions." If this is your initial reaction to this chapter, I urge you to reconsider. There is good evidence to suggest that people who lack expertise in a given area of endeavor tend to overestimate their abilities relative to their peers, while those in the top quartile generally underestimate their relative abilities.[4] It's always tempting to dismiss statistical data as pertaining to "other people." Please don't kid yourself. Even if your business track record consists of a string of successes, you are probably susceptible to many of the biases that afflict us all. The experiments cited here show that when it comes to dealing with probabilities and uncertainties, most people (and that includes you and me) make irrational – or at least inconsistent – decisions. It's not just the weak, the biased, and the math-impaired who do this – it is all of us.

Milgram's Experiments

In the early sixties, Stanley Milgram of Yale University was fascinated by the horrible treatment of concentration camp victims by German soldiers in World War II. He conducted a series of experiments in which pairs of subjects were told that Milgram was doing a study on how well people learned things when they were punished by electric shocks for incorrect answers.[5] One subject was the tester; the other was the test-taker. The test-taker had electrodes attached to his body. The tester would ask questions, and whenever the test-taker got an answer wrong, the tester would administer an electric shock. With each wrong answer, the voltage was increased.

Except that it was all a deception. There was only one subject: the tester. The "test-taker" was in on the scam, an actor who intentionally got answers wrong. The electric shock was very mild, of course, regardless of the apparent voltage setting, but the test-taker would cry out in pain when the tester pushed the button at higher settings (the only reason that there was any shock at all was because the actor had to know when the tester had pushed the button). Milgram wanted to see just how far people would go.

The results were disturbing, to say the least. Most people went all the way up into the "danger" zone on the voltage control, even when the test-taker screamed in pain, begged them to stop, and/or claimed to have a heart condition. This was especially true when the authority figure conducting the experiment remained in the room and reassured the tester that everything was fine.

Milgram's experiments showed that it wasn't that the Germans were mindless automatons or immoral beasts. Under the right circumstances, most people would perform horrible acts if told to do so by a strong authority figure. We could no longer claim that there was something "wrong" with the thousands of Germans who obeyed orders to torture innocents.

As you might guess, many people rejected Milgram's results. Studies like these tell us about ourselves, and sometimes we don't like what we hear. Many people simply refused to believe that they and others like them would ever behave the way Milgram's subjects did. This is really just the Lake Wobegon syndrome, in which everyone believes that they are above average.

Likewise, it's easy for us to convince ourselves that the results detailed in this chapter don't apply to us, that we are somehow superior to the subjects of these experiments. Don't be too quick to jump to this conclusion. Like Milgram's experiments, the research covered in this chapter passes the tests of statistical validity and is not easily rationalized away. If you've worked your way up the corporate ladder, you may very well be better than average at assessing uncertain situations rationally.

But we're all human.

Knowing this can help you fight your natural tendencies and make better decisions. But the natural tendencies will still be there.

Points to Ponder

During the Cuban Missile Crisis of 1962, President John F. Kennedy is reported to have intentionally kept his opinions to himself during the early days of the crisis, and even stayed away from some early meetings during which alternative courses of action were being generated and discussed.

- ♦ Why would he do this?
- ♦ How do you think this tactic may have contributed to the successful resolution of the problem?
- ♦ How might business leaders adopt this technique?

Endnotes

1. Morse, Gardiner. "Decisions and Desire," *Harvard Business Review*, Vol. 84, No. 1, pp. 42-51, 2006.

2. The original article contained in Kahneman and Tversky's book is from *Journal of Economic Behavior and Organization*, 1, Richard H. Thaler, "Toward a Positive Theory of Consumer Choice," 39-60, 1980.

3. Bazerman, Max H. and Chugh, Dolly. "Decisions Without Blinders," *Harvard Business Review*, Vol. 84, No. 1, pp. 88-97, 2006.

4. Kruger, Justin and Dunning, David. "Unskilled and Unaware of It: How Difficulties in Recognizing One's Own Incompetence Lead to Inflated Self-Assessments," *Journal of Personality and Social Psychology* Vol. 77, No. 6: 1121-1134, 1999.

5. Milgram, S. "Behavior Study of Obedience," *Journal of Abnormal and Social Psychology* 67:371-8, 1963.

"O to be self-balanced for contingencies,
To confront night, storms, hunger, ridicule, accidents,
rebuffs, as the trees and animals do."
– Walt Whitman

". . . they fail to work out contingency plans to cope with
foreseeable setbacks that could endanger the overall success
of their chosen course."
– Irving L. Janis in 1971, describing teams that have
fallen into groupthink

7

Contingent Probabilities

We have seen that people have numerous biases and weak-
nesses when it comes to assessing and interpreting probabili-
ties. But the problem can be even more basic than that. With
contingent probabilities (i.e., situations in which the probability
of one event depends on the outcome of another), there are fun-
damental rules of math that must be obeyed. A surprising per-
centage of the time, they aren't. This chapter is designed to
warn you and arm you against such mathematical transgres-
sions.

This chapter is a short diversion into a probability-related issue that is problematic in many companies: contingent probabilities. Kahneman and Tversky didn't (to my knowledge) perform experiments specifically targeting this subject, but it is an excellent example of a concept that is commonly misunderstood in business and with which many human beings struggle. I have seen clients estimate probabilities of occurrence for future events under different scenarios that were mathematically impossible. If the probability estimated for Scenario 1 was accurate, the probability estimated for Scenario 2 *could not* be correct. The clients didn't realize this because they did not understand the rules for contingent probabilities.

This may seem like an obscure subject for an executive-level discussion (and this chapter may read a bit more slowly than previous chapters). But the concepts are important and merit discussion.

Paired Product Launches

This is the scenario: you're launching a new product, A, this year. You believe that A has a 60% probability of being successful. You plan to launch a related product, B, next year. You believe that if A is successful, it will increase the probability of success for B. However, you must make the decision whether to launch B before you know whether or not A is successful. Your best estimate of the probability of success for B after A has been launched is 20%. However, if A is successful, your estimate of the chance of success for B increases to 40%.

Have you ever been in a situation like this? Most of us have. Business consists of an endless stream of projects, many of which are interrelated enough to where the outcome of one will cause us to change our opinions about the probable outcome of another.

There's just one problem with the scenario as described above: it's mathematically impossible. If we currently assess the probability of success for A at 60%, and that for B (after A is launched) at 20%, there is no way that B's probability of

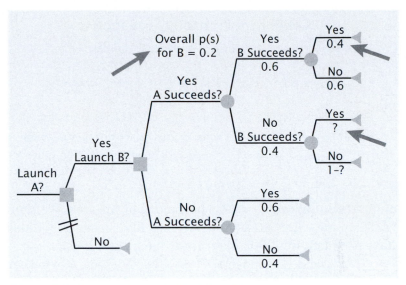

Figure 7.1. Product Launch Decision Tree

success can increase to 40%, regardless of how big a smash hit A is.

There are several ways to analyze situations like this. We are going to use two: decision trees and overlapping areas.

Figure 7.1 shows the decision tree associated with this scenario. Events on decision trees run chronologically from left to right. The first event is the decision to launch product A (represented by the square node on the far left). We have already made the decision to launch A, so the lower half of the tree – the part associated with deciding not to launch A – has been eliminated (as shown by the double-strike across that branch of the tree).

The second event is the decision to launch product B (the next square node). We can decide to do so (and move diagonally up), or not to do so (and move diagonally down).

Regardless of which choice we make, the next event is the resolution of the uncertainty regarding whether A will be successful (represented by a circle). A has a probability of success of 60%, as shown. If we decide not to launch B, this is the

Contingent Probability Equation

The equation for this contingent probability problem is:

$$p(B) = p(B \mid A) \times p(A) + p(B \mid notA) \times p(notA), \text{ where:}$$

$p(X)$ is the probability of X occurring (or in this case, succeeding);
$p(notX)$ is the probability of X not occurring (or not succeeding);
$p(X \mid Y)$ is the probability of X occurring given that Y occurs.

only remaining event, so this is the end of the tree. We then realize some value associated with the final scenario (values have been left off of this diagram to simplify things).

If we decide to launch B, then after we find out whether or not A is successful, we will find out whether or not B is successful (as represented by the next circles in the upper part of the tree).

We have specified two probabilities of success for B: the overall probability of success given that we have launched A (the "0.2" on the diagram), and the probability of success for B given that A is a success (the "0.4" in the upper-right part of the tree). We have not specified the probability of success for B given the failure of A, so there is a question mark on the tree in that position.

This is where our problem becomes apparent. The three probabilities of success for product B (the ones with arrows pointing at them) are not independent of each other. The over-all probability of success for B (which is 0.2) must equal the probability of success for B given the success of A (which is 0.4) times the probability of success for A (0.6), plus the probability of success for B given the failure of A (the "?") times the probability of failure for A (0.4).

This is impossible, regardless of what probability we put in place of the "?". The first half of the equation alone (0.4 x 0.6) exceeds the estimated overall probability of success for B (0.2). We would need a negative probability in place of the "?", which is impossible. If we truly believe that the current probability of success for B is 20%, there is no way that that probability can rise to 40%, even if A is a fantastic success.

The same conclusion can be reached by looking at overlapping areas that represent the probabilities in question, as shown in figures 7.2, 7.3, and 7.4.[1] In each figure, the large box (the boundary of the figure) represents the set of all of the possible things that could happen in the world – i.e., 100% of the future scenarios we believe could occur after A is launched. Every point in the box represents a different scenario, and every possible combination of events that we believe to be possible in the future is represented by a point somewhere in this box. This is our current "world view," so to speak, complete with uncertainty about what will happen.

The shaded area "A" represents all of the scenarios in which A is successful, and as expected, it covers 60% of the total area. If we believe A to have a 60% chance of success, then 60% of the possible futures in our world view must include a successful A. Likewise, the shaded area "B" represents all of the cases in which B is successful after A is launched – 20% of the total area. (If we decide not to launch B, then shaded area "B" obviously goes away. But in order to analyze the probabilities, we hypothesize for now that B will be launched.)

Before attempting to solve our specific problem, let's look at a couple of end-member scenarios. In Figure 7.2, there is no overlap between the shaded areas "A" and "B" (under no circumstances are both A and B successful). They are mutually exclusive in this world view; if A is successful, B most certainly will not be, and vice-versa. So in this scenario, the success of A would definitely tell us something about the probability of success for B. If A is successful, B's probability of success drops to zero.

To understand this, we need to realize that if A is successful, the shaded area "A" becomes our new view of all the possible things that could happen in the world. We can safely eliminate all previous possibilities that did not include A's success, because we now know that it is successful. The shaded

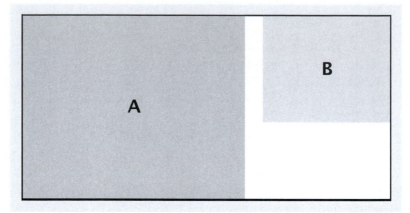

Figure 7.2. Probabilities of A and B – No Overlap

area "A" becomes our new world view, given the success of A. This is analogous to choosing the "A is successful" branch of our decision tree.

This is the way projects work; our broad view of the uncertain outcome becomes narrower as uncertainties are resolved and the success or failure of each project is determined. Since there are no cases in Figure 7.2 in which both A and B are successful – i.e., there is no point in the box covered by both shaded area "A" and shaded area "B"– the success of A means the certain failure of B in this scenario. They are mutually exclusive.

What about the scenario in which A and B are completely independent of each other (i.e. we believe that the success or failure of A tells us nothing about B's chances for success)? What does the world view look like?

The case in which A and B are independent is shown in Figure 7.3. Area "A" still covers 60% of the world view, and area "B" still covers 20%, but now there is a 12% overlap (60% x 20%). What does this say about the probability of success for B, *given the success of A*? If A is successful, what percent of our new world view will be covered by the shaded area "B"? This is an easy calculation. If A is successful, our new world view becomes the shaded area "A". What percent of the shaded area "A" is covered by the shaded area "B"? Well, A repre-

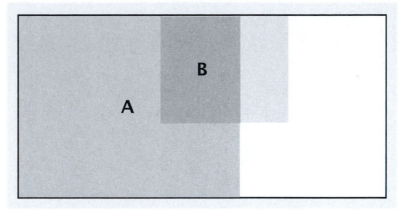

Figure 7.3. Probabilities of A and B if Independent

sents 60% of the current world view, and the overlapping area represents 12% of the current world view. 12% / 60% = 20%.

Thus, if A is successful, B still has a 20% chance of success (12% / 60%). The part of area "B" sticking out to the right of area "A" is 8% of our world view (B's 20% minus the 12% overlap). The space not covered by area "A" is 40% (since area "A" covers 60%). Thus, if A fails, the probability of success for B is 8% / 40% = 20% once again.

So whether A succeeds or fails, B's probability of success remains at 20%. The converse is also true: whether B succeeds or fails, A's probability of success remains at 60%. This is the definition of two independent events.

But this is not the situation we wanted to describe in our original problem. We want to show a case in which A's success actually increases B's probability of success – and increases it to 40%.

No problem – just rearrange our shaded areas (without changing their size) so as to increase the overlap. As we do this, the portion of A covered by B increases— i.e., the probability of success for B *given the success of A* increases (and of course, if we decrease the overlap, the probability of success for B given the success of A decreases).

But there *is* a problem: no matter how we rearrange these shaded areas, we can't make the shaded area "B" cover forty

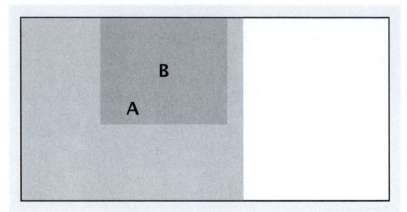

Figure 7.4. Probabilities of A and B with Maximum Overlap

percent of the shaded area "A". It just isn't big enough. In fact, even with total overlap (Figure 7.4), the probability of success for B, given the success of A, is only 33% (20% / 60%). This is the maximum possible probability of success for B, given the success of A. Estimating a higher probability than this violates basic rules of mathematics and statistics.

Thus, both of the approaches used to analyze the problem yield the same result (as they should). As a manager, the point to remember is: we can't just arbitrarily set probabilities to whatever we'd like them to be. There are certain rules of mathematics that must be obeyed. In this case, if we truly believe that A has a 60% chance of success and B has a 20% chance of success after we launch A, then the maximum chance of success for B *given the success of A* is 33%. Conversely, if we truly believe that A has a 60% chance of success and the chance of success for B *given the success of A* will be 40%, then we have to believe that B has *at least* a 24% chance of success after we launch A. No other values are logically consistent.

The Gold Mine

Let's look at another scenario: You own a mining company planning to dig for gold in an area where a rich vein is believed to run some distance below the surface. You've iden-

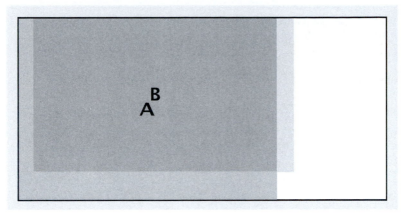

Figure 7.5. Given Successful A, B's Probability is 80%

tified two prospective locations, A and B. The probability of finding the vein at location A is estimated to be 70%. The probability of finding it at location B is estimated to be 60%. If the vein is found at location A, that will be a positive sign for the area, and the probability of finding it at location B increases to 80%; if the vein is not found at location A, however, the probability of finding it at location B stays at 60%.

Any problems with this? Yes, but for a different reason. In this case, it's easy to accommodate the first contingent probability – i.e., having the probability of finding the vein at location B jump to 80% in the event of a successful A (see Figure 7.5 and Figure 7.6).

Most of the probabilities here work out – shaded area "A" covers 70% of the world view, area "B" covers 60%, and the overlap area covers 80% of area "A." The problem comes with the last requirement – that if the vein of gold is not found at A, the probability of success at location B should remain at 60%. If the vein is absent at A, the area that is *not* covered by shaded area "A" becomes our new world view (because we can eliminate all cases in which the vein is found at A). Clearly, the little strip of shaded area "B" that sticks out beyond area "A" does not cover 60% of the entire area to the right of "A". Therefore, given the failure of A, the probability of finding the vein at B cannot remain at 60%.

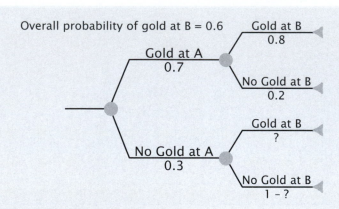

Figure 7.6. Gold Mining Tree

Gold Mining Decision Tree

Figure 7.6 shows how to look at the gold mining question using a simple decision tree. The overall probability of finding gold at location B is 60%, and this probability rises to 80% if gold if found at location A. So far, so good. The problem comes with the third requirement – that if gold is not found at A, the probability of finding it at B should remain at 60% (which is why there is a "?" in the tree).

As in the product launch case, the three probabilities specified for finding gold at B are related. The overall probability of finding gold at B must equal the probability of finding gold at B given that it is found at A times the probability of finding gold at A, plus the probability of finding gold at B given that gold is absent at A times the probability of gold being absent at A.

So 60% = 80% x 70% + ? x 30%. Solving for "?" reveals that the probability of finding gold at B given that it is not found at A must be 13.3%.

We can calculate what it should be. If area "B" covers 80% of area "A", the overlap must be 56% of the current world view (80% x 70%). Since area "B" is 60%, this leaves an area of "B" sticking out to the right of area "A" equal to 4% of the current world view (60% – 56%). Since area "A" covers 70% of the world view, the area to the right of it – the "vein is not found at A" area – must cover 30%. So if the vein is not found at A, that 30% becomes our new world view, and out of that 30%, 4% is covered by area "B". 4% / 30% = 13.3; thus, the probability of finding the vein at B *given that the vein is absent at A* is 13.3%.

This *has* to be true, given the probabilities specified for A, B, and B-given-A-succeeds. Again, we can't just set probabilities to whatever we'd like them to be.

This is likely to make a huge difference in your plans. Had you simply accepted the original assessment – that if the vein is absent at A, there is still a 60% probability of finding it at B – you may very well have decided to proceed with development at B, even if A proved disappointing. Armed with the correct contingent probabilities, however, you would know that if the vein is not found at A, there is only about a 13% probability of finding it at B – a much riskier prospect. You would probably make a very different decision about developing B.

The "overlapping area" approach to analyzing contingent probabilities is really just set theory, which used to be taught in elementary school math classes.[2] The problem is many people have forgotten it. But in a world of probabilities and uncertainties – in the world of *business* – it's important to be logically consistent. We need to dust off our understanding of these concepts if we want to run our companies in an optimal way.

Although the ideas in this chapter may seem esoteric, they are important. In business, we make plans and spend money based on our assessments of probabilities of success. All too often, our assessments don't make mathematical sense.

Making sure that they do can sometimes be as simple as drawing a few rectangles on a piece of paper.

Points to Ponder

In the "Gold Mine" case, the key uncertainty (whether or not the gold vein is present at one or more locations) is a state-of-nature – either gold is there or it is not. There is nothing we can do to change its presence or absence.

In the "Product Launch" case, however, launching Product A might completely change the market for Product B (i.e.

the probability of success for B might be very different from what it would be if A had not been launched). This is why I specified that the decision to launch A *has alrady been made*, and all probabilities are estimated with this as given.

Suppose we had not yet made the decision to launch A. How would our analysis change? The probability of success for B would now not only be dependent on the success or fail-ure of A (which is an uncertainty), but would also depend on whether or not we choose to launch A at all (a decision). How does this complicate the issue?

Hint: draw the tree!

Lottery Statistics

My statistics professor in graduate school (we'll call him "Dr. M") told a story about when he had some work done on his car. By way of making conversation, the mechanic asked him what he did for a living, and Dr. M replied, "I teach statistics."

The man's face lit up. "You do?" he asked, excitedly. This was not the reaction Dr. M had come to expect when people learned of his area of expertise. The mechanic went on to exclaim, "You can help me with the lottery!"

Despite Dr. M's protests to the contrary, the man insisted on sharing several drawers' full of data he had collected on the lottery – how frequently each number had been called, how frequently each number had been played, which combinations had been played most often, which combinations had won recently, etc. The mechanic was sure that Dr. M could use statistical analysis to dis-cern subtle patterns that would bring him riches beyond his wildest dreams.

Number Combination	How Many People Played This Combination
7 – 14 – 21 – 28 – 35 – 42	16,532
1 – 2 – 3 – 4 – 5 – 6	14,981
3 – 6 – 9 – 12 – 15 – 18	13,344
4 – 9 – 22 – 36 – 37 – 43	11,257

Table 7.1. Most Popular Combinations Played in the Lottery One Week

Needless to say, it didn't quite work out that way. Dr. M did, however, gain an excellent data set – namely, the list of how frequently each number had been called as a part of a winning combination in the past. Those of us in his class were to analyze this set to determine if the uneven distribution of frequencies for the different numbers was statistically significant. To the surprise of no one, it was not. The variation in the frequencies was well within the range of random variance.

What was interesting, though, was the list of the combinations of numbers that had been played by the largest number of people on one randomly selected week. Table 7.1 gives the top four six-number combinations and the number of people who played them (I don't recall all of these numbers exactly, but Table 7.1 is close enough to illustrate the key points).

The first and third combinations in the table – the "7s" and "3s" – aren't too surprising. Many people believe sevens and threes to be lucky. The second and fourth entries, however, are certainly unexpected.

Dr. M found the second combination to be extremely amusing. "Here we have people who know enough about statistics to realize that 1-2-3-4-5-6 has just as good a chance of winning as any other combination," he said. "What's funny is I'm sure that every one of the 14,000-plus people who played this combination thought, "No one else would ever play 1-2-3-4-5-6. If I win this thing, I won't have to share it with anybody!"

The fourth combination was puzzling until Dr. M told us that that had been the winning combination the previous week. So again, you had people who knew enough about contingent probabilities to realize that the numbers called on any given week are not contingent on what was called the previous week. Despite winning the week before, these numbers had just as good a chance of being called as any other six-number combination. And again, everyone who played this combination was undoubtedly thinking, "No one else would ever play this combination!"

So maybe there's more statistical literacy – if not common sense – out there than we think.

Incidentally, there is one tactic you *can* use to minimize the number of people with whom you will have to share the lottery if you win: choose numbers greater than 31. Many people use dates (birthdays, anniversaries, etc.) when choosing lottery numbers.

Endnotes

1. Bill Haskett was the first person I ever saw use the technique of overlapping areas to get these concepts across, and Bob Winkler used it even earlier in his 1972 book. I do not claim originality for this approach.

2. Again, Bill Haskett was the first person I heard to point this out.

"I feel like a fugitive from th' law of averages."
– Caption from a cartoon by Bill Mauldin

8

Which Number Do You Want?

Decisions are best made with an understanding of the full range of probable outcomes. However, there is no avoiding the need for numbers: single values (usually statistics) that represent one measure or another. But different statistics serve different purposes and have different advantages and disadvantages. This chapter investigates those advantages and disadvantages, and provides you with the information you need to choose your numbers wisely.

DEFINITIONS

Measurements of Central Tendency:

The mean, median, and mode. If one number must be put forward to represent an entire distribution, these three statistics are the ones most commonly used. Some are more useful than others.

Mean:

The probability-weighted average of all values in the output distribution. The mean is the Expected Value (EV) of the distribution – i.e., if you were to take on a large number of projects with identical NPV probability curves, you would, on average, realize the mean value NPV for each project done (even though you are unlikely to realize the exact mean value on any of the projects).

Median:

Also called the p_{50} value. That value about which there is a 50/50 probability of the parameter coming in higher or lower.

Mode:

The value that has the highest probability of occurrence. This is usually the least useful of all measures of central tendency when dealing with output distributions. The mode only has real meaning for discrete distributions; continuous distributions have no true mode, although they often look like they do. This is because values are usually carried to many decimal places, so the probability of any one value occurring more than once is nil. Remember: continuous frequency distributions output from Monte Carlo simulations are *histograms*; the height of the curve shows the probability of having a value *between two points* on the x-axis, not the probability of having a certain, specific value. Even when the curve is drawn as a smooth line, it's really just a very fine histogram.

So the apparent "mode" on a continuous distribution is almost useless (my colleague Bill Haskett calls the mode "evil," which is probably only a slight exaggeration). It gives you an idea of the neighborhood in which most of the values will lie, but that's about it.

Standard Deviation:

A commonly used measure of how wide a probability distribution is (i.e., how broad the uncertainty is), often represented by the

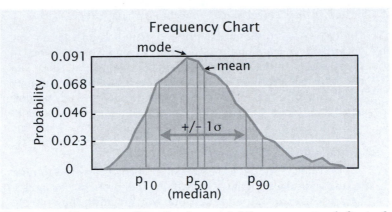

Figure 8.1. *Frequency Distribution with Measurements of Central Tendency and Standard Deviation*

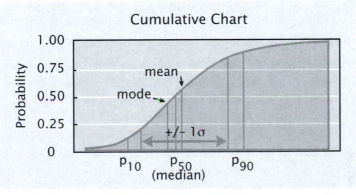

Figure 8.2. *Cumulative Distribution with Measurements of Central Tendency and Standard Deviation*

symbol σ (sigma). On a Normal distribution (i.e., a "bell curve"):

♦   about 68% of all values lie within +/- 1 standard deviation of the mean,

♦   about 95% lie within +/- 2 standard deviations, and

♦   nearly all values (99.7%) lie within +/- 3 standard deviations of the mean.

As σ gets bigger, the distribution gets broader and flatter; as σ decreases, the curve becomes more like a spike, with almost all values clustered around the mean and very little uncertainty. (See Figures 8.1 and 8.2).

The Central Limit Theorem (CLT) and the Portfolio Effect:

The CLT refers to the fact that if you sample a population, the uncertainty concerning the population's mean will be Normal in shape and centered on the mean of your sample set. The theorem provides a formula to calculate how broad the uncertainty curve should be (the standard deviation will be inversely proportional to the square root of the number of samples that you take). The more samples you take, the more confident you are that the entire population's mean lies somewhere close to your sample set's mean.

In common usage, the CLT is often incorrectly used to refer to stochastically summing a large number of probabilistic inputs. This results in an output distribution which tends to be centered around the sum of the input distributions' means and Normal in shape with a standard deviation that is narrower (as a percentage of the mean) than that of the input distributions. This assumes that the inputs are at least partially independent and that more than one input contributes significantly to the uncertainty of the output.

This phenomenon (sometimes called the "portfolio effect") has nothing to do with the CLT but is still important. Summing a large number of input distributions generally results in a narrow, normal-shaped output distribution centered on the sum of the means.

As the title of this book implies, most people want the number, not curves or ranges. And indeed, everyone has to come up with numbers eventually – after all, annual reports and earnings forecasts are full of them.

So which number do you choose? A probability distribution of the type that we've been discussing has a multitude of numbers that you can pull out – statistics, percentiles, etc. When the time comes to use a single value, which one is appropriate?

The answer (as it always is with a consultant) is, "It depends." In this case, it depends on what you want it for.

For most purposes, the mean (the probability-weighted average value of the curve) is the value of interest, for two reasons:

1) The mean is the Expected Value (EV), and as stated in Chapter 5, risk-neutral decision-making involves comparing the EVs of the alternatives. For most decisions,

An Eye-Catching Average

In 1984, Dr. Lawrence A. Simpson, Director of the Office of Career Planning and Placement at the University of Virginia, announced that graduates from the previous year with bachelor's degrees in Rhetoric and Communications Studies enjoyed an average starting salary of $55,000 per year (this is equivalent to approximately $100,000/yr in today's dollars).[1] Dr. Simpson said this with a wink (he knew what was coming next), but the statement was nevertheless true.

$55,000/year in 1983? The *average*? For people with a B.A. in Rhetoric and Communications? Newly minted engineers didn't earn half that amount. How can this be?

It's simple, really. You may remember a gentleman named Ralph Sampson: 7' 4" tall, first player selected in the National Basketball Association draft, and yes, a graduate of the University of Virginia in 1983 with a degree in Rhetoric and Communications Studies. All by itself, Mr. Sampson's multi-million dollar contract with the Houston Rockets was enough to skew the mean salary for all graduates with a similar degree up to $55,000 per year. In fact, it's probably a safe bet that Mr. Sampson's data point was the *only* one above the mean; the others were probably clustered significantly below the $55,000 mark.

The average height, incidentally, was over six feet tall.

therefore, the mean of a probability distribution or histogram is the statistic of greatest interest.

2) Means are additive. Sum up the means of the assets in a portfolio, and you'll get the mean of the entire portfolio. This doesn't hold true for any other statistic (not even the p_{50}). Thus, you should *expect* to get the sum of the means out of your portfolio of assets. In addition, if there's enough diversity and independence between assets, the portfolio effect will cause the overall portfolio curve to be fairly narrow on a percentage basis. Thus, even though you may not have much confidence that you will come within, say, +/– 5% of the mean on any individual asset, you may still be quite confident of staying within that range at the portfolio level.

Means, however, have their quirks. Probably the biggest problem is they are extremely sensitive to outliers – individual data points that lie far away from all others in the set. In a small town with 600 factory workers and one billionaire factory owner, the average net wealth per family will be well over a million dollars – hardly indicative of typical family life in that community. The average weight of a St. Bernard and nine Chihuahuas will probably be something close to 20 pounds, but that's not a very useful number for describing any of the dogs. With highly skewed distributions, means are not always the best statistic to use to characterize the set as a whole.

To understand why this is such a serious limitation, consider another "net wealth per family" situation: What would happen to the average wealth per family in your neighborhood if Bill Gates moved in down the street? Unless you live in a far swankier part of town than I do, average wealth would skyrocket a hundred-fold or more.

And yet, very little about the neighborhood has changed. The vast majority of the data points (families' wealth) are exactly what they were before Bill bought his summer cottage in your area. The local school might suddenly be blessed with all the computers it can handle, but in general, life would go on as before. The sudden discontinuity in average wealth would not be indicative of a significant change in the population as a whole. And remember, we're discussing which single value is the best one to *represent* the entire group. If the mean doesn't resemble a "typical" data point, its usefulness will be severely limited. And with highly skewed distributions, the mean usually will not be very "typical."

So what do we do? Many common data sets are, in fact, highly skewed. House prices, net assets for different companies, revenue streams from new movies – all are data populations with a very large number of low values, tapering down to a very small number of huge values. If means aren't very good for representing these populations, what statistic is?

In instances like these, if a single value is required to characterize the population, the median, or p_{50}, is often the statistic of choice. This is the value which fifty percent of the data points lie above, and fifty percent lie below. Since it makes no difference *how far* above or below the median the points lie, the median is far more resistant to undue influence by outliers.

So returning to the Bill Gates example, let's say that, prior to Bill's arrival, your neighborhood consisted of 100 families, and when they were ranked in order of total wealth, family number 50 was worth $1,000,000, and family number 51 was worth $950,000. The median wealth per family would be $975,000 (if a population has an even number of data points, the p_{50} is halfway between the two central points). After the Gates family's arrival, there would be 101 families, and the median would now be $1,000,000 (the center data point in the new, odd-numbered population) – an increase of only $25,000, or about 2.6%. This is far more indicative of the likely impact on the neighborhood of adding one very wealthy family.

This is why government statistics almost always refer to the *median* family income in Iowa, or the *median* house price in San Francisco. Means can jump up or down as a result of the addition or deletion of one or two extreme values. Medians are much more stable. If, for some reason, the median value of a distribution does jump or plummet, something very significant is going on.

So the median is often a logical statistic to use if you are concerned about the undue influence of a few outliers. It may also be the statistic of choice if you are taking a single shot at, say, funding a new high-risk start-up company. If you only plan to fund one start-up, it is unrealistic to expect returns greater than or equal to the mean of the returns realized on previous start-ups of a similar type. The median is more likely

*Pain of Regret

An even better way to think about this is in terms of what Bill Haskett calls the Probability of Regret and the Pain of Regret – i.e., how likely is it that things will turn out badly, and how bad is that likely to be (bearing in mind that a lost opportunity is painful, too). But that approach uses two metrics, and what we're discussing here is which metric to choose if you're forced to represent a probability range with a single value.

to be achieved or exceeded (and since more than 50% of start-ups fail completely, the median scenario would be the loss of your entire investment).*

However, if you plan to fund a *statistically significant* number of high-risk start-up companies over a period of time (or develop a statistically significant number of new drugs, etc.), the *mean* once again becomes the statistic of choice, regardless of how skewed the distribution is. This is because – as mentioned before and as we shall see in more detail later – when a large number of assets (or projects, or investment opportunities, etc.) are summed, the overall distribution tends to tighten up around the sum of the means of the individual assets.

Just remember: for very highly skewed distributions, the "statistically significant number" might prove to be very large, indeed. If one new drug out of a hundred makes a billion dollars for the company, and forty-nine out of a hundred just break even, and fifty out of a hundred lose $5 million, the EV of each drug of this type is $7.5 million. Very nice, indeed. But how many of these drugs do you need to have in your portfolio in order to be, say, 60% sure that you'll break even at the very least? As it ends up, you'd better have at least 92 such potential blockbusters in the pipeline. If you want 80% confidence, the number jumps to 161.

If you can't afford to lose money for a very long time, playing statistical roulette like this is a dangerous way to live.

This is the venture capitalist's game. You must choose wisely when funding new start-ups, and don't put all your eggs in one basket. In order to have any likelihood of a positive return, you must use the statistics to your advantage and invest in a number of different (i.e., independent) ventures. You must also be fairly ruthless about pulling the plug on losing projects – with so many more losers than winners, averaging even a slightly higher loss than necessary on the bad ones will kill your overall expected return.

However, if you choose wisely and repeat the process enough times, your overall return should be the sum of the mean values; the median becomes irrelevant. Thus, the mean is the appropriate statistic to use in this situation. For those who *can* afford to lose repeatedly, opportunities abound.

Of Medians and Men

Another tricky question is, "What statistic makes for an appropriate objective, goal, or production target for an asset team or business unit?" Assume that we've done our Monte Carlo analysis, we understand the probabilities associated with the range of possible outcomes, and we understand that the variance is due to uncertainties that are beyond the control of our employees. Nevertheless, people are more motivated when they are shooting for specific goals, and we would like to reward those teams that achieve their goals. Which number do we pull off the curve and set as a target for our team or business unit?

The answer here (to use a bit more consulting doublespeak) is that there is no correct answer – it's a management choice. Different numbers will have different effects, and each has its pros and cons.

Let's start with the mean. The one big advantage of using the mean is that it is neat and orderly. If each asset team's target is the mean of its distribution, then the sum of the individual team objectives will equal the overall business unit's objective (assuming the B.U.'s objective is the mean of the overall distribution). Likewise, letting the mean serve as the target is consistent with your planning efforts, since the mean (or Expected Value) is the number that should be used in making strategic business plans at the portfolio level.

But the mean has several drawbacks as a production target. First, it's not likely to be fair from team to team. One team with a fairly symmetrical distribution might have a 48% chance of exceeding the mean. Another team, working on a higher-risk asset with a more skewed distribution, may have only a 32% chance of beating their mean. Through no fault of their own, members of the second team are less likely than the first team to achieve their objective.

These percentages hint at the second drawback: most forecast distributions in business are skewed to the right, and as such, the mean is greater than the p_{50}. Thus, the majority of your teams will fall short. If that suits management's approach to handing out bonuses, fine, but it's probably not going to do much for morale. The best motivational goals are challenging, but reachable (Natemeyer and McMahon, page 138).[2] Put people in a position where they fail significantly more often than they succeed, and productivity tends to drop.

In fact, if motivating the troops is the driving force behind setting targets, there is evidence to indicate that people are most highly motivated to attain a goal which they have roughly a 50/50 chance of achieving. Set the goal at, say, the p_{20} (too easy), and there's no challenge to it. Set it at the p_{90} (too hard), and people won't even try. This is intuitively obvious, and can be confirmed just by watching someone shoot baskets by herself on a basketball court. She won't pour in lay-up after lay-up, nor will she try a bunch of nearly impossible shots. Subconsciously, she'll seek out shots that, on average, she has about a 50/50 chance of making. Why? Because those are the most interesting – the most *motivating*. Oh, she'll occasionally try a wild one from half-court. But almost regardless of skill level, most people usually end up making about half of the shots they attempt in situations like this.

Thus, the case for the median – the p_{50} – as a production target is based on the notion that this goal will provide maximum motivation for team members (and in general, it will). In addition, it's fair: everyone will have the same chance of achieving their goals.

But again, no target is perfect. Use the p_{50} as objectives for your asset teams and business units, and all of the plusses associated with the mean become minuses:

♦ The sum of your asset teams' p_{50} targets will not equal (and will usually be less than) the overall business unit's p_{50}.

- The sum of the team's targets will not be the appropriate value to use in the B.U. planning process.
- In addition, roughly half of your teams will fail to achieve their targets in any given year, and some may fail to do so for a number of years in a row, purely as a result of the randomness of an uncertain world.

So as I warned you, there is no simple answer to the question of setting goals or production targets. The issue really needs to be thought through for each individual situation, and customized to meet the circumstances and needs of local management.

That said, I usually recommend the p_{50} as a target at the project level and the mean as a target at the B.U. level. Yes, the sum of the teams' targets won't equal the B.U.'s target – so what? The B.U.'s mean will almost certainly be greater than the sum of the teams' p_{50}s, thus providing a bit of added incentive for everyone to keep on stretching, even if their team is having a banner year.

In fact, at the BU level, it really doesn't matter whether the p_{50} or the mean is chosen as the target – they're virtually the same number. Assuming your business unit has at least a dozen or so assets and/or projects of comparable size and uncertainty, by the time you sum them up, the overall curve will approach a Normal distribution (a "bell curve"). (The stochastic sum of a large number of distributions tends to become Normal, regardless of the shapes of the individual distributions.) Normal distributions are symmetrical; the p_{50} equals the mean. Yours won't quite be Normal, and therefore the mean and p_{50} won't quite be equal. But they'll be close.

A final thought to close this chapter: just because I have not come down strongly in favor of one statistic or another, don't get the impression that it doesn't matter. The question of which value best represents a probabilistic range is important. Analysts want numbers, not ranges – do you want to give them a number that is optimistic, to show confidence? Pessimistic, so you're sure you can reach it? Teams perform best with targets to shoot for – do you want them to be reached often, or rarely? We can only learn from the past if we track our results versus our predictions – which value(s) in the predicted range should we be tracking against? How far can we stray from these predictions before we should begin to worry that we're doing something wrong? If we intend to fund capital investments out of (uncertain) revenues next year, which value should we choose? How likely is it that we'll exceed that number? How large is the risk if we do?

Only through appropriate probabilistic assessments and intelligent selection of statistics can we answer these questions and run our businesses properly. Generating public enthusiasm for a new product line, rebuilding an under-performing business unit, planning a strategy to capture additional market share – each of these requires a *different* number. Only by understanding these concepts can executives choose the numbers that will help to accomplish what they are trying to do.

Points to Ponder

Nassim Taleb tells of being required to attend weekly "discussion meetings" when he was employed by a large New York investment house (Taleb, pp. 86-87). During one of these meetings, Taleb declared that (1) he had taken a short position on a large number of S&P 500 futures, thus betting that the market would go down, and (2) that, in his opinion, there was about a 70% probability that the market would go up over the coming week.

Were his two declarations consistent or inconsistent with each other? Why?

The Gulf of Mexico Group

An oil and gas company had several exploration groups, one of which focused on the Gulf of Mexico. The team had mapped a potentially very large accumulation, then bid on and won the lease for the acreage, and finally gained corporate approval to drill the well. As is usually the case in oil exploration, the probability of there being any hydrocarbons at all was less than 25%, and – if the well did make a discovery – the uncertainty range for how much oil might be in the trap was very broad.

The well did, indeed, find oil, and the initial estimate of the amount discovered was extremely close to the p_{50} value from the original uncertainty range. The team was ecstatic, as this was a very large discovery, and it had come in essentially as predicted. Kudos to the geologist for accuracy!

To make the situation even more festive, the company had a policy of rewarding large discoveries with bonuses. The manager of the group announced that everyone was required to attend a meeting the following morning. The buzz in the office was high.

It didn't last long. At the meeting the next day, the manager was obviously angry. "You found the p_{50}," he snarled. "We are not a p_{50} company; we are a p_{90} company." There would be no bonuses because the team had "only" found an amount close to the mid-point of the uncertainty range. Stunned, the team members wandered back to their offices.

From then on, a strange phenomenon occurred in the Gulf of Mexico group. They almost never generated any more large prospects. In areas where other companies were making substantial finds, this company's employees mapped only small-to-medium sized targets – ones on which the p_{90} value wasn't all that huge.

However, such mediocre prospects couldn't compete with those being generated by the company's other exploration groups, so the budget for Gulf of Mexico exploration was reduced. The company had better places to invest its money. Even when the group did manage to get funding for a prospect, competitors who saw higher potential invariably outbid them for the leases.

The Gulf of Mexico exploration group simply stopped finding significant new reserves for the company. Eventually, the company was taken over by a competitor.

This is a classic case of unintended consequences resulting from a manager's lack of understanding of basic concepts. You simply cannot expect your people to generate p_{90} results on average. By definition, the p_{90} is that value you expect to achieve or exceed only 10% of the time.

Faced with that impossible demand, this team took the logical route: they reduced their estimates, such that their new p_{90} estimates looked a lot like their old p_{50} estimates. This manager's ignorance caused a bias in the team's assessments that made future analyses conservative to the point of uselessness.

The results for the company were disastrous.

Endnotes

1. Sports Illustrated magazine, February 20, 1984 issue.

2. The original article contained in Natemeyer and McMahon's book is from *Organizational Dynamics*, Gary P. Latham and Edwin A. Locke, "Goal Setting – A Motivational Technique That Works," 1979.

"None of us really understands what's going on with all these numbers."
– David Stockman, speaking of the U.S. federal budget in 1981

9

Rolling Up the Numbers Without Getting Flattened

Performing probabilistic analyses on individual projects and assets is critical to managing those projects appropriately. However, budgets are allocated and strategic decisions are made at the portfolio level. In this chapter, we look at why dependencies between projects must be considered when summing the probability curves for multiple projects and assets. Higher degrees of dependency result in a wider range of possible results from a portfolio. This is critical, since it is at the portfolio level that management's tolerance for risk and uncertainty should be applied.

(In this book, "rolling up" the numbers refers to stochastically summing the results on individual assets to determine the result for the entire portfolio.)

We've taken a look at the role probabilistic analysis plays in managing individual assets and projects, and in considering pairs of projects that have some degree of interdependency. I've also shown that decision trees and/or the probability curves output by Monte Carlo analyses improve decision making versus considering only single deterministic values. But very few businesses are comprised of a single project or a pair of projects. In general, we have a number of assets and projects under management, and we're interested in maximizing the return on the group as a whole.

This is portfolio management, and it has been a very hot topic for many years now – and for good reason.

This is what value generation is all about: delivering consistent value to shareholders by investing in high-EV projects or assets. Some or many of these projects may be fairly risky. Our objective is to compile and manage the total portfolio to maximize the overall expected value and bring the overall risk level into line with the owners' tolerance for such risk.

Accomplishing this is much more involved than simply choosing the best alternative under each individual decision, or even choosing the EV-maximizing strategy for each individual project in a portfolio. What is best for an individual project or business unit is unlikely also to be optimal for the corporation as a whole (Allen, pages 62-63).

Effective portfolio management requires estimating economic metrics (EV, ROCE, short-term earnings, risk, etc.) for the entire corporate (or business unit) portfolio and comparing these metrics for each viable alternative strategy. This is a daunting task which requires the use of a solid, creative, consistent decision process (described briefly in Chapter 11 and in greater detail in the Nutt, Skinner, and Allen books in the bibliography).

One piece of the problem involves applying probabilistic methods to analyze your projects and assets, and then rolling up the results in such a way that you get meaningful, useful information at the portfolio level.

Many companies have stumbled while negotiating this path. There is no cookbook answer, but in this chapter I will convey a few key concepts and some potential pitfalls.

This will not be an in-depth treatment of portfolio management issues. A number of very good books already exist on the subject, including Michael Allen's.[1] Rather, in keeping with the purpose of this book (namely, providing the background needed to employ probabilistic thinking and stochastic analyses in your decision making), I have limited the scope to the problems and pitfalls associated with implementing probabilistic methodologies across one's company, and then deriving appropriate metrics and statistics to use when making decisions at the corporate (i.e., portfolio) level. I will explain some of the statistical quirks to watch out for and several issues that merit attention. After that, you can decide what works best in your specific situation.

The Portfolio Effect

Let's start with the good news: Generally speaking, a large portfolio of volatile assets (or investments, or projects) will have a narrower standard deviation *as a percentage of the mean* than will any individual asset within the portfolio. Note the italics. Many people erroneously believe that adding a new asset to a portfolio will reduce the standard deviation of the value curve of that portfolio. This is only true if there is a negative dependency between the new asset and the existing portfolio – a rare situation in most businesses. Adding a new project or asset to your existing portfolio will almost invariably *increase* the absolute uncertainty, but *decrease* the uncertainty as a percentage of the mean value of the portfolio (recall that this is referred to as the portfolio effect).

Small portfolios also benefit from this effect, but they are obviously more volatile than large portfolios. When a small software company announces a new "killer application," its stock price may jump several fold; if Microsoft makes a similar announcement, its stock price may not budge. On a percentage basis, the $p_{10} - p_{90}$ uncertainty around the value of

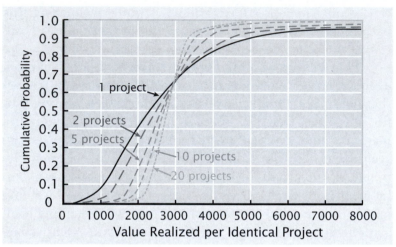

Figure 9.1. Portfolio Effect

Microsoft's portfolio of assets is far narrower than that of a small company.

But even if the low uncertainty at the portfolio level is only on a percentage basis, this is still good news. After all, percent return on investment is usually the metric of interest.

Figure 9.1 illustrates this concept (note that the graph shows value realized *per project* – not the total value of the portfolio). Each individual project used in the making of this graph has a cumulative probability curve identical to the flattest one – the curve associated with one asset. The projects are summed stochastically, using Monte Carlo simulation. As the number of projects increases, the curves become steeper, and the relative uncertainty of the overall portfolio decreases. This is why portfolios of assets are less volatile than individual assets.

This is also why, back in Chapter 5, I recommended pursuing the uncertain Project B over the certain Project A, provided you had many such projects to pursue. Project A had a sure NPV of $4 million; Project B had a success-case NPV of $25 million, a failure-case NPV of –$2 million, and a 28% probability of success. Any individual Project B, therefore, has a

72% probability of loss and the $p_{10} - p_{90}$ range of possible outcomes goes from −$2 million to $25 million. A portfolio of eight Project Bs, however, has only a 7% probability of loss, and an average-per-project $p_{10} - p_{90}$ range of outcomes that goes from $1.38 million to $11.5 million. On a percentage basis, the range of likely outcomes is much narrower. The portfolio is far less volatile than the individual project and carries a lower risk of losing money.

If this level of risk is acceptable, you should be pursuing your Project Bs. As I said in Chapter 5, the company's tolerance for uncertainty and risk should be implemented at the *corporate portfolio level*, not at the individual project level (or even the individual business unit level). Failure to do this – choosing "safe" projects with lower EVs because the company is unwilling to accept a significant probability of failure on any individual project – is a recipe for under performance at the corporate level.

This bears repeating. Just as surely as a poker player who would rather fold than risk losing a hand will never win a tournament, *a company that refuses to risk failure at the project level will, in the long run, be surpassed by competitors who are willing to take such risks.* Poker players routinely play hands on which they estimate their probability of winning to be less than 50%. If the size of the pot is large enough, they know that in the long run, they will come out ahead by playing those hands. The same philosophy – and mathematics – apply in business.

"Refusing to risk failure" is the exact same thing as "always demanding success." If the corporate culture expects success on all projects and punishes failure at this level, project managers will, of course, be strongly motivated to choose safe alternatives over uncertain ones, regardless of the relative expected values. And the company's return to shareholders will lag behind that of a company that truly understands uncertainty and implements its risk tolerance at the appropriate level.

Let's return to Figure 9.1. The curves cross at a common point. This is the mean value per project, and it doesn't change when you add up multiple projects. Remember: the sum of the means of a number of individual assets equals the mean of the sums, i.e., the mean value of the portfolio. Means are additive; no other measure of central tendency is.

Ideally, we should run probabilistic models on all of our individual assets simultaneously, sum them stochastically while they run, and use the output sum to represent the range of possible values of our portfolio. In a company with thousands of assets, however, this can bring even the most powerful of office computers to its knees (and exceed the capacity of most commercial Monte Carlo simulation software, too).

So we proceed in stages. The output curves for individual assets are summed stochastically at the Business Unit level, the Business Units' output curves are summed up to the Division level, and Divisions' curves are summed up to the Corporate level (just like the deterministic case). However, there is a trap.

Dependencies and Correlations

One of the biggest difficulties facing portfolio managers is how best to incorporate dependencies between assets and/or projects into their models. This is done by estimating (or if possible, measuring) the correlation factors between key inputs to the models and applying these factors when running the models. Failure to do this will almost always result in an output distribution that is too narrow – that is, the range of possible outcomes is underestimated. The upside scenario is too pessimistic, and the downside case is too optimistic. This can be dangerous at the corporate level, where decisions are often made on the assumption that, for instance, gross revenue over the next five years is highly likely to be greater than X (say, with a 90% probability). If you've overestimated X, you may be risking financial distress.

In Figure 9.2, for instance, the steepest curve is similar to the corresponding curve in Figure 9.1. It represents a port-

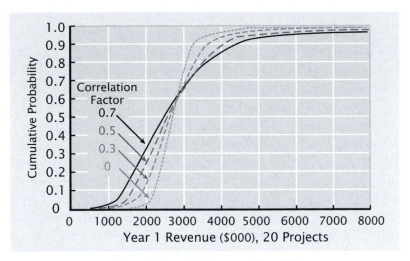

Figure 9.2. The Effect of Correlation on a Portfolio

folio of twenty identical *independent* projects (this graph, however, shows total portfolio revenue for Year One rather than
NPV per project). If there are, in fact, positive dependencies
between projects, the curve flattens significantly (as shown)
as the correlation factor becomes stronger.

This has major ramifications for budgeting. If you are
planning a capital spending program to be funded by existing
revenues and you want to be 90% certain you can afford the
program, you would choose the p_{10} value off the curve and use
that value as your conservative estimate for revenue from
these projects.

But which curve do you choose? If the projects are truly
independent, the p_{10} from the steep curve, about $2.2 million,
should be used. If the projects are fairly strongly correlated,
the appropriate p_{10} comes from the flattest curve, with a value
of about $1.4 million. Which value is appropriate? It can be
difficult to tell, because answering that question involves estimating the degree of dependency between the projects being summed.

Unfortunately, there is no one-size-fits-all solution to the
problem of dependencies and correlations. Assets with com-

mon input parameters and/or shared risk factors or dependencies should be summed with some degree of correlation applied, and those without these features should generally be summed independently. The problem is knowing which assets are which, and how strong the correlations should be.

To simplify things, some companies assume a high degree of dependency between assets within a business unit (erring on the side of caution when rolling the numbers up to the BU level), and then assume total independence when summing the Business Units' curves to the corporate level (which helps to mitigate the conservativeness of the BU-level roll-ups). There is some logic to this; after all, Business Units are usually organized based on some kind of similarity between assets. This might be geographic location (the Far East BU), product line (the Printers and Faxes BU), or whatever makes sense for that company. Since the assets and projects within the BU all have something in common, it's likely that they will share some dependencies. Conversely, the dependencies between different Business Units are likely to be weaker (not always – different BUs might have common suppliers, for example – but usually this is the case). So different Business Units' forecasts and values are probably more appropriately summed independently.

I'd like to offer a more complete answer, but in truth, each case requires an approach that is appropriate for the size of the company, the number of assets, and the detail needed to make a good set of decisions. As the decision maker, you need to be aware of the issue and have some level of understanding about what your financial modelers and planners are doing. Ideally, your understanding should be good enough to allow you to have an informed opinion regarding just how strong the various correlations should be, at least on a qualitative level (strong/moderate/weak/non-existent). You are likely to have a better big-picture view of these concepts than your modelers have, and your perspective should be a key factor in deciding how strong the correlations should be.

That is the bad news. The good news is that you can gain insight into your situation without getting the correlations exactly right. Roll up your portfolio using a global correlation factor of 0.4 between projects, and then again using a factor of 0.5, and you probably won't see a significant difference in the outcomes. The important thing is to apply a moderate correlation factor if you think the situation calls for one, not to calculate exactly what the numerical value of that correlation factor should be.

Therefore, I encourage my clients to make their best estimates and apply correlations where they think appropriate. The results will certainly be more realistic than they would be if they ignored correlations entirely.

Points to Ponder

I have made the case that a company's risk tolerance should be implemented at the corporate portfolio level and that individual projects should generally be judged on a risk-neutral basis.

How would a company's corporate culture have to change to accommodate this approach successfully? How might a company's employee compensation mechanisms have to be changed?

Endnotes

1. This book and Mr. Allen's cover some very similar subjects, but with different focuses. Mr. Allen's book centers on portfolio management, and covers related subjects only to the extent necessary to get the portfolio concepts across to his reader. My purpose is to teach readers how to use probabilistic methods in multiple ways throughout their companies; portfolio management is one such application, and I'll go into only as much detail as needed to make my points clear.

"The time which we have at our disposal every day is
elastic. . ."
– Marcel Proust

"Lost time is never found again."
– Benjamin Franklin

10

Late and Over Budget –
Project Management
Issues

Project managers fight several statistical phenomena against which they almost always lose: near-critical-path tasks, right-skewed distributions, and the MAIMS effect (Money Allocated Is Money Spent). The result is projects that consistently take longer and cost more than expected. Understanding these phenomena won't make them go away, but it will enable managers to plan and budget for projects appropriately, manage expectations, and avoid dangerous traps.

The methods used to manage a portfolio of individual assets (discussed in Chapter 9) also can be used to manage a project's individual tasks. In fact, some of the graphs in this chapter closely resemble those in the previous chapter, and with good reason: they are constructed in the same way. Some of the conclusions, however, may be surprising or even distressing.

Projects that take longer than expected and run over budget (sometimes *way* over budget) are endemic in the business world. Consider construction of new retail stores, upgrading of highway interchanges, installation of new water and sewage facilities, building new manufacturing facilities – all fail to meet the predicted timetable more often than not. Today, it is almost a cliché that *any* large-scale project is likely to miss its target deadline and exceed its budget.

As a result, "fudging" is common. An expanded time estimate is entered for most major tasks just in case problems are encountered, and the all-purpose "contingency" item makes its appearance in almost every Gantt chart and cost estimate. There is a reason for this: lots of things can go wrong on a major project. Weather alone is a wild card that affects outdoor projects. Yet even with contingency tacked on and major task durations estimated on the high side, many projects still exceed the predicted time (and budget, which generally goes hand-in-hand with time). Moreover, we usually have no way of predicting how likely it is that a given project will meet its milestones and/or overall timetable.

Why should this be? Are project managers and crews really this incompetent? Does Murphy's Law have something to do with it?

The short answer is "No" (although I wouldn't rule out Murphy's Law entirely). Project teams are generally staffed with trained professionals and skilled laborers who know their jobs well. They're just fighting forces against which they rarely win.

Near-Critical-Path Activities

Most major projects run multiple tasks in parallel. Often, a subsequent task cannot begin until all of the preceding parallel tasks have been completed. As a simple example, imagine building a house and having plumbers running pipes, electricians running wires, and air conditioning specialists running duct work in the walls. Theoretically, all of these workers can be active on the house simultaneously (especially if it's a big house so they can work on different parts and not get in each other's way). However, the dry wall cannot be installed until all of these tasks have been completed.

In situations like this, the longest of the parallel tasks becomes part of the critical path for the project (the "critical path" is the string of tasks that determines the overall time it will take to complete the project). Some amount of delay on non-critical-path tasks can be tolerated, but any delay on critical-path tasks directly results in delay on the project as a whole (note that the time to complete the whole project is usually one of the key "numbers" that executives want).

Now consider Figure 10.1 – a portion of a Gantt chart for a hypothetical major project. Five tasks are running in parallel and the longest of these – task C – is on the critical path. The other four tasks (B, D, E, and F) are all nearly as long as C, but not quite. If the length of each task is the estimated p_{50} in each case, what is the probability that all five tasks will be completed in the time allotted?*

Let's break it down and start with the easiest one: what is the probability that task C will be completed within the time allotted? Fifty percent, of course – we just said that the

*Time Uncertainty

There is, of course, uncertainty surrounding any estimate of time needed to complete a task. Regardless of what number is put forward, there is some probability that the actual time needed will be less, and some probability that the actual time needed will be more. In this case, we are assuming that the values entered for each task represent the planner's best estimate of the p_{50}.

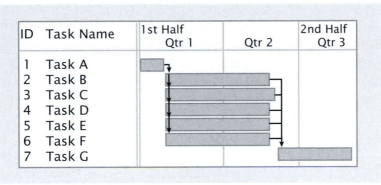

ID	Task Name	1st Half Qtr 1	Qtr 2	2nd Half Qtr 3
1	Task A			
2	Task B			
3	Task C			
4	Task D			
5	Task E			
6	Task F			
7	Task G			

Figure 10.1. Gantt Chart With Parallel Tasks

allocated time represents our best estimate of the p_{50}. So half the time, task C will take less time than predicted, and half the time it will take more (for simplicity's sake, tasks that are completed exactly on time are considered to have been completed in less than the time allotted).

Now, what about tasks B, D, E, and F? In each case, the allotted time (which is the p_{50}, remember) is only slightly less than the allotted time for task C. This means a little bit of delay can be tolerated, but not much. If any one of these tasks ends up taking longer than task C, it replaces C on the critical path and delays the project.

So what is the probability that task B will be completed in less time than the amount allocated for task C? We cannot tell the exact probability by looking at this Gantt chart alone, but it is almost certainly only slightly higher than 50% (since B has a 50% chance of taking less than its allotted time, and its allotted time is only slightly less than that for task C). This would also be the case for tasks D, E, and F.

A subtle problem begins to reveal itself. With sequential tasks, delay on one task can sometimes be compensated for by speeding up a later task. Not so with parallel tasks: in order for the overall project to avoid delay, *all five* of these tasks must be completed in less than the time allotted for task C. What is the probability of this happening?

Assuming the tasks are independent of each other (i.e., delay on one says nothing about the probability of delay on any other), the probability of all five tasks being completed within the time allocated for task C is simply the product of the five individual probabilities. For tasks B, D, E, and F, this probability is slightly higher than 50% – let's say 55%. For task C, the probability is 50% exactly. 50% x 55% x 55% x 55% x 55% = 4.6%.

In other words, this part of the project has less than a 5% chance of meeting its deadline, despite the fact that each individual task has a 50% chance of coming in on time. The project team is probably doomed to fail before the first two pieces of wood have been nailed together.

This problem is exacerbated by most project managers' tendency to focus almost exclusively on critical-path tasks (in this case, Task C). The probability that Task B, for instance, will take less than the time allotted for Task C is about 55%. Conversely, the probability that Task B will exceed the time allotted for Task C is about 45%. However, this assumes that Task B is given the proper attention. If Task B goes largely ignored, this probability can easily jump from 45% to 50% or more – a higher probability than that for Task C.

Even if this doesn't happen – even if the project manager watches all five tasks with equal concern – the probability is higher that one or more of the four near-critical tasks (B, D, E, and F) will end up exceeding the time allotted for Task C than it is for Task C exceeding its time. The former probability is about 91% (1 – [0.55 x 0.55 x 0.55 x 0.55]); the latter probability is only 50%. This is because there are four of the near-critical tasks and only one critical one. It is far more likely that one (or more) of the four will have problems than it is that Task C, specifically, will have problems.

Modeling the project schedule stochastically will not just give you a better idea of the range of possible values for the duration of the project. It will also allow you to identify tasks which are *not* on the critical path in the deterministic case, but which have a significant probability of ending up on the critical path. You can then focus resources on these tasks and try to ensure that they don't slip. This type of analysis is easily missed when projects are planned deterministically.

The Gantt chart shown is admittedly just an example. It may not be very common to have five parallel tasks that are almost the same duration. However, even with only two parallel tasks – let's say B and C – the probability of both coming in without delay is only about 28% (55% x 50%). Moreover, we're only looking at one set of parallel tasks here. A large project will have dozens of sets of parallel tasks, some with five or more tasks, some with only two or three, some that are nearly uniform in length, some that are of vastly different lengths. The total effect gets multiplied, and the result is near-certain delay to the overall project.

The Portfolio Effect and Right-Skewed Probability Distributions

Even without parallel tasks, most projects are unlikely to finish on schedule if a "most likely" or a p_{50} is used for the allotted time for each individual task and these are summed to develop the overall project schedule. The reason is interaction between the portfolio effect and skewed uncertainties.

There is uncertainty surrounding any estimate of how long a task will take. A simple task that has been done many times before should have a small uncertainty range. With large, complex tasks, however, the uncertainty becomes very significant, especially if we're depending on factors beyond our control (like the weather).

For most tasks in most projects, this uncertainty distribution is skewed to the right – that is, the distribution will show a much longer tail extending off to the right than it will show on the left (see Figure 10.2). If everything goes well and our good-luck charms work, we might finish a task 20% or 30% ahead of schedule. But if a gale hits, key parts never show up at the work site, and the electricians' union strikes, task completion could be delayed by 200%, 300%, or more. There is a physical limit to how quickly a task can be done,

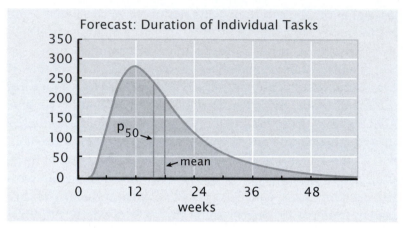

Figure 10.2. Probability Distribution for Length of Individual
    Task

but there is no upper limit to how long it might take. Thus, the range of possible values for the time to complete this task ranges from only a little below our predicted value to way above our predicted value. This is what the probability distribution in Figure 10.2 shows. The most likely time needed for this task is in the range of 8 to 16 weeks, and it could be as low as 5 or 6 weeks. But it could also be as high as 40 or 45 weeks.

So why should right-skewed distributions spell problems for projects? The answer can be found by using Monte Carlo simulation to sum a large number of such distributions. To demonstrate this phenomenon, we'll look at a project with twenty tasks, each with an identical uncertainty distribution (for simplicity's sake) and running sequentially – i.e., no parallel tasks (Figure 10.3). Let's also assume that if we were estimating the time for this project deterministically (the way it's usually done, with single values for each input rather than a probability distribution), the "best estimate" that would be entered into the Gantt chart for each task is equal to the p_{50} of that task's uncertainty distribution (in this case, 16 weeks). And there's one final assumption: the tasks are independent

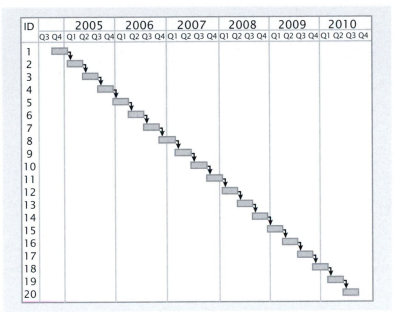

ID	2005		2006				2007				2008				2009				2010			
	Q3	Q4	Q1	Q2	Q3	Q4	Q1	Q2	Q3	Q4	Q1	Q2	Q3	Q4	Q1	Q2	Q3	Q4	Q1	Q2	Q3	Q4

Figure 10.3. Gantt Chart of Twenty Sequential Tasks

of each other, or nearly so (how long one task takes has no effect on how long other tasks will take).

The output cumulative distribution curve from running a Monte Carlo simulation for this project is shown in Figure 10.4. What does this tell us about the probability that we'll complete this project in less time than deterministically predicted? Where does the sum of all the p_{50} estimates – which would be our "best guess" estimate – fall on this curve?

The sum of the p_{50} estimates is 320 weeks, which corresponds to a probability of 14% on the curve. In other words, if we use estimates for individual tasks that we think we have a 50/50 chance of achieving in each case, our overall probability of achieving this timetable is only 14%. We are highly likely to miss our deadline.

This happens because:

1) If you sum a number of uncertain items stochastically, the relative range of the output distribution tends to tighten up around the sum of the means of the inputs

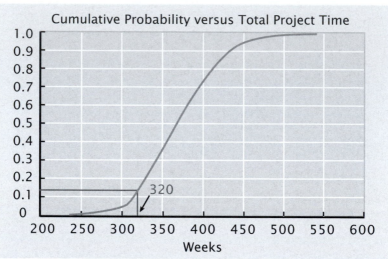

Figure 10.4. Total Project Time Cumulative Probability Distribution, 20 Tasks

(this is the portfolio effect mentioned in Chapter 9).

2) The mean of a right-skewed distribution is higher than the p_{50} (see Figure 10.2 again).*

What does this mean in plain English? Better yet, let's look at a picture. In Figure 10.5, we start with a single task, and then add more and more tasks to the project and watch what happens to the overall time needed. These plots have been normalized so they can be compared with each other directly. The x-axis shows the average time taken for each task, rather than the total time for the whole project. Note that – just as happened in Chapter 9 when more assets were added to our portfolio – as more tasks are added to our project, the curve becomes steeper. The range of possible values for average time per task becomes narrower.

*Problems with the "Most Likely"

Note that not only is the mean higher than the p_{50} in right-skewed distributions, but the p_{50} is higher than the mode, or "most likely" – the highest point on the curve. Thus, if the estimates you've put into your Gantt chart are "most likely" values rather than p_{50} estimates, you are even less likely to meet your predicted deadline.

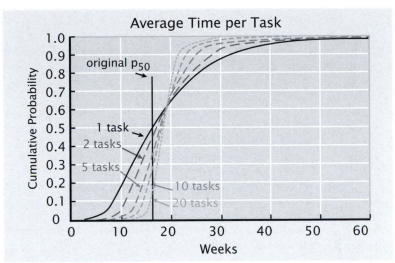

Figure 10.5. Average Time per Task, Different Numbers of Tasks
    Summed

Just as in the portfolio case, the pivot point about which the curves become steeper is the mean, not the original p_{50}. As a result, as more and more tasks are added, the probability that the average time taken per task will be less than or equal to the original p_{50} drops from 50% to 44%, to 35%, to 25%, to 14%. Eventually, the probability of averaging the original p_{50} value becomes negligible. We're almost certain to exceed our predicted timetable.

This example uses twenty identical independent tasks to simplify the demonstration, but the result is the same regardless of whether the tasks are of varying length or not. As long as the uncertainty distributions are right-skewed (which is almost always the case) and the tasks are at least partially independent of each other, as more tasks are added, the probability of staying on the deterministic schedule shrinks to the point of becoming extremely unlikely.

To put it bluntly, deterministic scheduling for major projects isn't good enough. Two phenomena – the effect of parallel tasks with nearly the same length and the portfolio effect as applied to right-skewed distributions – combine to virtually ensure failure to meet a deterministic timetable.

Preemptive Resourcing – A Success Story

A commodities company was engaged in a major project in South America. One key piece of this project was building a large processing plant, which was actually proceeding well ahead of schedule in the early stages. Needless to say, this was very good news and was shared with the company's financial creditors.

To be on the safe side, though, the company performed a stochastic analysis of the remaining portion of the schedule. They input ranges of values and probability distributions for the durations associated with all of the remaining tasks, and ran a Monte Carlo simulation. The results were sobering.

Despite the exceptional early progress, the project was not likely to meet the deterministic deadline set in the original schedule. Several potential bottlenecks appeared in the probabilistic analysis that were originally unnoticed because they were not on the deterministic critical path. However, when uncertainty was taken into account and modeled correctly, these tasks had a significant probability of ending up on the critical path and delaying the project.

Thus forewarned, the company took two key steps. First, they notified their bankers of the situation and warned them of the possibility of future delays. Second, they hired additional laborers for those key tasks that had been identified, thus reducing the predicted duration distributions and mitigating anticipated bottlenecks. They were able to anticipate problems ahead of time and took steps to prevent delays before they occurred.

The project finished on time and under budget. The creditors were pleased.

We've examined each effect individually here, but they combine and multiply on large, complex projects to the point where it is common to have less than a 1% chance of meeting the deterministic schedule for the overall project.

Historically, companies have either arbitrarily adjusted the numbers upward or included contingency items in order to accommodate the possibility that unforeseen problems will delay the project. This is better than nothing, but not by much. We are still left with no idea about the *probabilities* that we'll achieve our milestones, or how likely it is that we'll finish the new factory in time to start production before the fall season, or whether we'll avoid contract penalties for failing to meet deadlines. In order to manage our projects competently, we must employ stochastic scheduling (and an ever-increasing number of project managers are doing just that).

With stochastic scheduling (using Monte Carlo simulation), curves like the one in Figure 10.4 give us far more realistic estimates of overall project length, how much it's likely to cost, and the probability that we will meet our deadlines. This is a significant improvement over simply summing best estimates for the time needed for each task. Further, modern stochastic project scheduling software enables us to identify key tasks (those that are most likely to cause delay and/or cost overruns) whether they are on the critical path or not.

This allows for more thorough and efficient project management. By knowing ahead of time which tasks have the greatest potential to delay the project, managers can preemptively plan to concentrate money and manpower on these areas, thereby improving the probability of a successful project (i.e., one that finishes on time and on budget).

Getting MAIMed

Even with stochastic scheduling, project costs are affected by an additional factor: the dreaded MAIMS effect. "Money Allocated Is Money Spent." This refers to the strong tendency of project teams (and sub-teams) to spend whatever money is allocated to them, regardless of the amount. Even when fortune smiles on them and luck goes their way, at the end of the day it is rare for a team of people to give back a significant portion of whatever money was allocated to them (Kujawski and Alvaro, page 3). They may choose higher quality materials, or they may double- and triple-check some items, or they may decide to ship parts overnight to increase the probability of an early finish to the project. But they will find a use for whatever monetary expenditure has been approved.

Figures 10.6 and 10.7 show why this is a problem. Suppose you've been a conscientious project manager and have modeled your schedule and costs with Monte Carlo simulation. The cumulative probability curve for the cost of some group of sub-tasks in your project – call this Sub-Group A – is

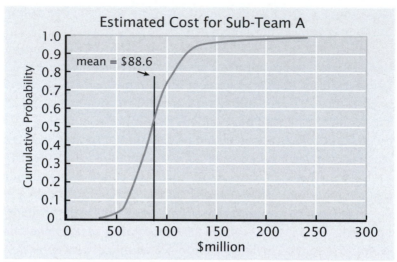

Figure 10.6. Cumulative Probability Curve for Sub-Team A's
Costs

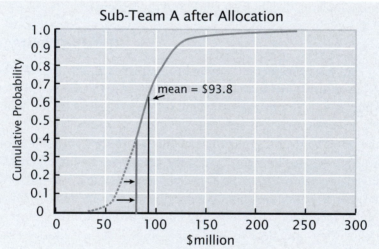

Figure 10.7. The Cost Curve Is Truncated at the Allocated Amount

shown in Figure 10.6, along with the mean cost (the expected
value).

Say you decide to allocate $80 million to the team (the
p_{40} amount). You fully realize that there's a 60% probability
that they will exceed this amount, but that's okay – you are
holding a contingency fund for the overall project, and those

sub-teams that need extra funds will be able to come to you for them.

But remember the MAIMS effect: Money Allocated Is Money Spent. If you allocate $80 million to this team, you can essentially forget about the probability that the team will spend less than that. In those instances in which lady luck smiles on them and they would be on the lower part of the curve, they'll find a way to spend something close to the full amount you allocated (otherwise, you probably won't give them as much next time!). This truncates the curve on the downside at the allocated amount (Figure 10.7).

But look what happens to the mean in this case: it increases from $88.6 million to $93.8 million.

The very act of allocating funds has decreased the probability that you will stay within your budget! This is more than just an ironic twist. It's a very real characteristic of the dynamic, interactive nature of estimating costs, budgeting, allocating funds, and bidding on work.

There is no magical way to eliminate the MAIMS effect, but the paper by Kujawski and Alvaro referenced in the bibliography describes a good approach to understanding and managing it. The key is to capture the interactive nature of uncertainties and budgeting decisions when you model the project cost, and then incorporate the insights gained into your project management and execution plans. You will be able to put contingency plans in place for when the unexpected occurs (and prevent problems from occurring in the first place) far better than you would have with the usual deterministic approach to project management.

The fact is, you cannot begin to cope with these issues if you are creating your project schedules deterministically. Anyone who is serious about realistically forecasting project schedules and costs, anticipating potential trouble spots, and taking action to mitigate against likely problems (in other words, truly *managing* major projects, rather than just monitoring them) should be using some type of Monte Carlo simulation methodology to plan and analyze projects. It's the best way to avoid "late and over budget" syndrome.

Points to Ponder

How might a project manager mitigate the first two phenomena (near-critical-path tasks and right-skewed task duration uncertainties) described in this chapter?

What other problems or issues might also cause a project to miss its target deadline?

". . . whereas all experiences are of the past, all decisions are about the future."
– Kenneth Boulding

". . . Pleasure and revenge have ears more deaf than adders to the voice of any true decision."
– William Shakespeare, <u>Troilus and Cressida</u>, Act II, Scene 2

11

What It's All About: Decisions

The probabilistic analysis techniques described in this book add value only if they help us to make better decisions. In this chapter, we put such analyses into the context of a solid decision-making process. Without such a process to ensure that the appropriate analyses (and only the appropriate analyses) are performed, that all critical data are included in the analyses, and that the results are incorporated into a forward plan that actually gets implemented, we are likely to waste valuable time crunching numbers and performing evaluations that add no value.

DEFINITIONS: Decision Analysis (DA) Terms

Facts:

These are known quantities (or at least known within a fairly narrow range). An example might be the agreed selling price for a commodity in a contract that has already been negotiated and signed.

Uncertainties:

These are quantities that are currently unknown, *and cannot be known for certain until sometime in the future* (usually well after the decision under consideration has been made). An example might be the market share your new software will command in North America the year after it's rolled out. You'll never know what this is until after the fact. A key characteristic is that uncertainties are *out of our control.*

Uncertainty should not be confused with ambiguity. Ambiguity refers to complexity or lack of clarity in purpose or meaning, and often comes into play with objectives (see below). With most uncertainties, the meaning is perfectly clear – it's just the value that is unknown.

Decisions:

Irrevocable actions that commit resources to one course of action or another. An example might be signing a contract to begin construction of a plant with the capacity to manufacture 200 motorcycles per day. Key characteristics are:

1) Decisions are entirely within our control. Circumstances and events may put us into a position in which only one decision is reasonable or sensible, but ultimately, the decision is our choice.
2) Decisions cannot be reversed or revoked without some penalty or loss. If they can be, then you haven't really made a decision yet.

Objectives:

Goals; what you're trying to accomplish by embarking on whatever course of action you're considering. An example might be to maximize the return on investment to shareholders, or to provide employment opportunities in the country in which you are operating. Ambiguous, conflicting, and/or hidden objectives are a common source of problems – and even failure – in business projects.

Let's return to the issue of holding managers strictly accountable for their business units' results (brought up in Chapter 5). Intuitively, this has a good feel to it – after all, what better way to eliminate favoritism, cronyism, nepotism, and all those other bad -isms than to tie reward firmly to results? It also appeals to the "stand up and take it like a man" culture – no excuses will be accepted.

But is this really sensible, let alone fair? Isn't it possible (downright likely?) that we will at least occasionally end up rewarding good fortune (rather than managerial brilliance) and punishing a perfectly competent team leader whose only fault was taking a reasonable risk, and losing? What message does this send to the troops?

The fact is, good decisions don't always lead to good outcomes, and bad decisions don't always lead to bad outcomes. Companies that made major investments in Iran in 1978 had no way of knowing that a revolution with ramifications for the entire world would occur the following year, and that most of their Iranian assets would be lost. Conversely, buying a lottery ticket is, by any objective measure, a bad decision – but for a few lucky individuals, the result is fantastic.

R. Richard Ritti presents an interesting perspective on this issue in his book, *The Ropes to Skip and the Ropes to Know*. "The folklore of every company contains accounts of heroic decision makers, stalwarts who made crucial decisions under conditions of great uncertainty and were right. And they did this time and time again... Admiring such heroic decision makers makes about as much sense as admiring the heroic pennies that come up heads in each of the twenty tries of the usual introductory probability theory example" (Ritti, pages 103-104). A bit harsh, perhaps, but there's a kernel of truth here.

There are literally millions of decision-makers in various businesses all around the globe. Even if we are all completely clueless and flip a coin each time we're faced with a tough problem, statistically, a few of us are going to be right almost every time. So is Jack Welch really a genius? Warren Buffett? Peter Lynch? How about Richard Branson?

Now, don't get me wrong; these are obviously very talented men, and I have tremendous respect for them. I have a feeling that at some intuitive level, they are better than most at sorting through complex uncertainties and identifying the key elements that require their attention. Jack Welch's grasp of big-picture strategy is obviously exceptional. Warren Buffett's integrity alone allows him to make deals that many others cannot, simply because people trust him. Peter Lynch brought an excellent combination of consistent methodology and common sense to picking stocks. Richard Branson appears to have an incredible intuition for identifying large-scale trends. But I hope each of these gentlemen would have the honesty to admit that good fortune also played a role in their successes.

The point is that there are things in this world that we cannot know for sure *and cannot control*. One of my favorite quotes from participants in my courses is, "My boss (or boss's boss) says that she wants 90% confidence of achieving the p_{50} result." This is ridiculous. No amount of hard work, brainstorming, extra diligence, or long hours can cause the price of steel to remain constant, the dollar/ringgit exchange rate to go down, the results of a clinical trial to be positive, or the demand for ski boots to go up next winter. If your best assessment with today's data is that you have a 50/50 chance of a project's NPV being greater than $10 million, there is nothing you can do to ensure that next year, $10 million will represent the p_{10} estimate. By definition, the p_{50} is that value about which we believe we have a 50% chance of falling short of it, and a 50% chance of exceeding it. You cannot choose to be at a certain point on your probability curve.

Combatting Randomness

But wait a minute – does this mean we're all helpless, tossed at random by the capricious fates? Didn't Louis Pasteur say that chance favors the prepared mind? There must be *something* we can do to improve our odds.

Of course there is: we can make good decisions. Unlike uncertainties, decisions are well within our control. And the decisions we make today change the shapes of the probability curves associated with the uncertainties we must deal with tomorrow (which then influence the decisions we make tomorrow, which then change the shapes...etc. – it's an iterative process). A detailed treatment of decision-making processes is beyond the scope of this book, and a number of good books on the subject already exist (two of which are listed in the bibliography). But any discussion of probabilistic methods must tie in with decision making – after all, the reason we go to all the trouble to understand uncertainties is to make better decisions.

Often, we make decisions *specifically* to change the shapes of our uncertainty probability distributions (like when we decide to conduct marketing surveys, collect information on competitor production capacity, or do research into the high-temperature viability of a new non-stick coating for pots and pans). Usually, we're trying to reduce the range of an uncertainty distribution. I'll go into these types of situations in more detail in Chapter 12, which deals with the value of information.

There is nothing contradictory about these last two paragraphs and the statement four paragraphs ago that there is no way to ensure that this year's p_{50} will become next year's p_{10}. We make decisions to gather data and/or eliminate potential courses of action from consideration, and as a result, our uncertainties' probability curves change. But we cannot control exactly *how* they change (although they generally become narrower with increased information, indicating a reduced range of possibilities). New data may reveal that the project is far *poorer* than originally thought, not better. The curve will probably become narrower and the range of uncertainty will be reduced – but this year's p_{50} may become next year's p_{97}. If this weren't the case – if there were actions we could take that we knew would cause the p_{50} value to jump – then this would not be our current estimate of the p_{50}.

A Brief Sojourn Into the World of Decision Analysis

Good decisions don't guarantee good outcomes, and bad decisions don't guarantee bad outcomes. But good decisions certainly increase the odds of good outcomes (and vice-versa for bad decisions).

So how do you ensure good decisions? One key ingredient is a methodical decision-making process that:

♦ uncovers all stakeholders' interests and goals,
♦ identifies the key uncertainties and decisions to be made,
♦ generates creative alternative approaches,
♦ evaluates these alternatives in such a way as to identify the key risks and uncertainties, and then
♦ implements the approach with the highest chance of achieving the objective(s) (Nutt pages 41-44).

This process is commonly called Decision Analysis, or "DA" (Michael Allen calls it the "dialogue process" in his book). When implemented correctly, DA not only yields a higher probability of good results, it decreases the time needed to arrive at a decision.

Figure 11.1 is a very high-level depiction of the decision analysis process.

The first three stages of the process involve uncovering, clarifying, and organizing all of the myriad issues that typically surround a major project. Only after this has been done can the team begin to think creatively about how best to proceed.

The development of strategic alternatives in the fourth stage of the process requires the team to stretch their imaginations. These alternatives usually have titles like "Dominate the Competition," "Conservative," "First to Market," etc. Each one should be logically consistent and possible (not necessarily probable, but possible – something you actually *could* do, and *might* do if the argument is compelling enough). Each one should also be distinctly different from the others. The

Raise Issues	Uncover objectives, decisions, uncertainties, and facts
Clarify Goals	Eliminate ambiguity in objectives; deal with conflicting objectives
Identify Boundaries	Separate key focus decisions from those that can wait until later
Generate Alternatives	Develop creative strategies
Evaluate Alternatives	Identify key uncertainties as value drivers; value-of-information analysis; develop an optimal hybrid strategy
Implement Optimal Strategy	Plan for flexibility; capture option value; contingency planning; continue the decision process

Figure 11.1. The Decision Analysis Process

idea is to capture as much of the "decision space" as possible – i.e., look at the entire range of options available. Only in this way can the effect of each individual decision be assessed, as well as the uncertainties that may drive value up or down significantly.

The objective is not to evaluate every possible permutation of decisions. Evaluating such a huge number of combinations would be a waste of time. If you've created five or six logical, distinct strategies that – between them – manage to explore the vast majority of the possible choices for the focus decisions at hand, your evaluation will give you the insight you need to choose an optimal way forward.

The probabilistic methods discussed in this book come into play in the fifth stage of the process, the evaluation stage. The uncertainties that have been identified during the DA process become the key input components to the stochastic models that are built to evaluate your strategies.

Finding the Dominant Objective

A consumer product manufacturer had always perceived a trade-off between meeting the customers' requirements and keeping costs down. Limiting the number of basic "design platforms" kept costs in check, but often prevented engineers from developing new products that had all of the features customers wanted. Allowing the engineers to improvise as they saw fit enabled them to customize new products to meet demand, but raised operating costs.

A stochastic analysis of the key value drivers revealed that potential revenue from meeting customers' desires simply dwarfed the costs associated with achieving this goal. The entire company philosophy changed from "There is a compromise to be made between meeting customer demands and keeping costs down" to "We *will* meet customer requirements. Now, what is the most cost-effective way of accomplishing this?"

This is a common revelation. On at least 80% of the tornado charts I have seen, the uncertainties at the top – the key value drivers that really make a difference in profitability – are on the revenue side of the equation, not the cost side. Yet costs are what most managers focus on. Why? There are usually two reasons.

First, compensation is often tied to keeping costs down. If your bonus depends on staying under budget, you'll stay under budget. What gets rewarded gets done.

Second, we have more control over cost-related uncertainties than we do over revenue uncertainties. We can *decide* to buy cheaper materials, use fewer people, invest in more efficient manufacturing plants, etc., but we cannot *decide* to have a high market share, high demand for our product, or a high price (price sustainability is an uncertainty).

Nevertheless, many executives and managers are "cost wise and revenue foolish." There *are* actions we can take to increase the probability of higher revenues, and meeting customer desires is a huge one.

Japanese automakers are an example. Toyota's operational efficiency is the envy of the industry, but – in my opinion – that is a secondary reason for the company's profitability. The primary reason is their ever-increasing market share. What drives their market share up? Certainly not their operational efficiency – the buying public couldn't care less about things like that. The fact that Toyota sells reliable, comfortable, fuel-efficient, stylish cars – i.e., they give their customers what they want – *that* is what has given them their market share and their climbing revenues. The company's efficient, low-cost operations just ensure that a higher portion of those revenues are retained as profit.

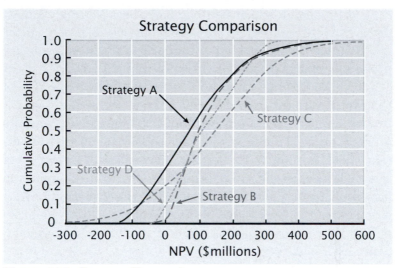

Figure 11.2. Strategy Comparison

A model must be built for each strategic alternative, estimating the measures-of-value (like NPV) from the input
parameters. This is nothing new – people have been doing
this for years with spreadsheets. The leap forward in understanding the upside potential and downside risks associated
with each strategy comes from using Monte Carlo simulation
and decision trees to create ranges and probability curves for
each measure-of-value. A typical output looks like Figure 11.2.

The x-axis shows NPV, and the y-axis shows the probability of a given strategy yielding an NPV less than or equal
to the corresponding x-axis value. So, for example, Strategy
C has about a 62% chance of resulting in an NPV less than
$200 million (and conversely, a 38% chance of an NPV greater
than that amount). Just go straight up from the $200 million
point to where it hits curve C, and then look on the y-axis to
see the corresponding cumulative probability.

Therefore, curves to the right are good; those to the left
are not as good. But these curves cross each other, sometimes
more than once. How do we make sense of this?

At this point, which strategy looks best is largely a matter of opinion. Strategy A is probably out of contention – after all, Strategy B has an equal or higher value across the entire probability range (Curve B is always even with or to the right of Curve A). Strategy C is the winner over the upper 70% of the probability range, but it also carries the second-highest probability of a negative NPV (about 20% likelihood) and the largest potential monetary loss (possibly well over $100 million – look how far to the left the lower part of Curve C extends). It's a high-potential, high-risk strategy. A comparison between Strategy B and Strategy D shows something interesting: over the lowest 40% and the highest 10% of the probability range, Strategy B is superior; in between, however, Strategy D looks better.

So which do you choose?

The answer is usually "none of the above." At this point, a smart project team will try to glean insight from the analysis. What drives the wide variance in value for Strategy C? Is there some information we might acquire to narrow the uncertainty? Why does Strategy D have several inflection points along the curve, indicating a bimodal or multi-modal distribution? What gives Strategy B such a low probability of a negative NPV – and whatever it is, can we pull it out and apply it to, say, Strategy C?

From questions like these, hybrid strategies are born that are better than any of the ones considered to date. This is a key point: at this stage of the analysis, we are not trying to choose between strategies A, B, C, and D. We evaluate these strategies to gain insight into what drives value on this project, what needs further investigation, what can be ignored for now, and – finally – what an optimal strategy might look like.

You might ask, "Why not put together an optimal strategy in the first place? Why waste time with multiple approaches that "explore the decision space"? The answer is that except in the simplest of situations, you won't *know* what the optimal strategy should look like until you've completed the analysis. The insights gained from analyzing the results of these distinctly different strategic approaches to the problem are what *enable* you to design an optimal strategy.

However, no amount of analysis – Monte Carlo or otherwise – can make up for an earlier poor job of uncovering objectives, focusing on key decisions, and generating creative alternative strategies. These activities (often called "framing") are crucial to a good decision analysis process. Get this right, and the quantitative analysis will usually fall into place. Get this wrong, and you're in trouble before you've even opened a spreadsheet.

I also must re-emphasize what I said about Monte Carlo simulation in an earlier chapter: it's garbage in, garbage out, and it's easier to hide the garbage in a stochastic model than in a deterministic one. After you've completed framing, getting high-quality inputs for your quantitative analysis is critical. The uncertainty ranges can and often will be broad, but they must represent the opinions of the best experts available.

You will sometimes hear people advocate conservatism when assessing projects or assets. Estimate the costs high and the revenues low (just to be safe), and you'll be fine. This is very dangerous. If you consistently underestimate the value of your projects, you will lose out to competitors who (accurately) see greater value and are willing to pay more. Your capital expenses will stay low, but your revenue stream will slowly dissipate. You'll put yourself out of business, slowly but surely.

Decision makers are most effective when they have unbiased and valid information. Only by portraying upside potential and downside risk as accurately as possible can you put yourself in a position to choose optimal strategies.

The Option Play

Decision Analysis often yields another big payoff: it enables you to identify options and to estimate the value of those options. By "options" I mean flexibility in one's future plans – e.g., the ability to get out of a contract if certain circumstances

Capturing Option Value

A major manufacturer was examining the possibility of installing laser welding in its plants (which numbered in the dozens). There seemed to be high potential value if all went well, but the technology was new at the time, and no one really knew if it would be worth the risk and disruption of implementation. Management was reluctant to commit to such a large change when success was by no means certain.

The logjam was broken by reframing the problem as an option. Proponents of laser welding requested funding to test the new technique in one or two plants, committing only to a technology R&D and testing program, as opposed to full implementation. If the tests proved successful, the company could proceed to full implementation with confidence (and reap the considerable rewards). If the tests were unsuccessful, the project would be dropped with no further investment. Probabilities were estimated for these two scenarios, and an expected value was calculated.

The new EV – which now incorporated the option value inherent in the situation – was very impressive, and the downside risk was minimal. The project was approved without controversy.

This may sound like common sense – *of course* you would pilot a new process or technology on a small scale before implementing it across your entire business. But sometimes it takes a shift in management's point of view to see the range of options they have. Further, many companies fail to grasp the full value of such option-bearing projects. They will test the technology, but only if they believe it is likely to work. If the probability of success is low, many companies won't proceed with the pilot, regardless of how high the upside potential might be.

For instance, suppose the laser welding process in this example was estimated to have only a 20% probability of working well enough to warrant the disruption to manufacturing (all of the probabilities and values given here are fictitious – they have nothing to do with the real laser welding case). If this process were implemented across all of the plants and worked well, it would add $650 million in value; if it failed or didn't work very well, it would reduce value by $300 million. Implementing this technology would therefore have an expected value of –$110 million ($650 million x 20% – $300 million x 80%). Clearly a bad idea.

But suppose the process can be piloted in a couple of plants for a cost of $30 million. There is still only a 20% chance that the technology will work well, so the most likely result is a loss of $30 million. But if it does work, you still capture almost all of the upside value ($650 million, less the $30 million cost of the pilot). The expected value in this case is $100 million ($620 million x 20% – $30 million x

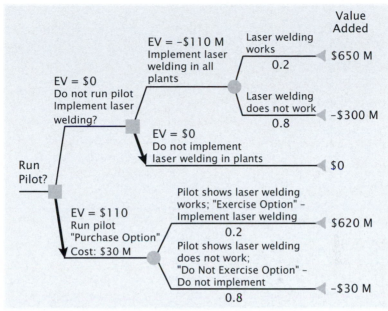

Figure 11.3. Decision Tree for Laser Welding Pilot

80%). The decision tree in Figure 11.3 demonstrates this result (recall that the EV at any uncertainty node – a circle – is the probability-weighted average of the possible outcomes; the EV at a decision node – a square – is the most favorable option – as indicated by the arrows – since we get to choose). The smart thing to do is to proceed with the pilot, even though you believe it to be four times as likely to fail as to succeed. If you take this approach every time, the few that succeed will more than pay for the ones that don't.

Viewing and evaluating pilots as options is a way to capture this upside potential and incorporate its value into our decision-making process. It's another way to gain competitive advantage.

arise, the option to change your mind and buy office space rather than rent, or the flexibility to double your production capacity on short notice if initial sales look promising. Just as a call option on a stock gives you the right (but not the obligation) to purchase the stock at a set price for a certain period of time, options in business (sometimes called real options) give you the ability (but not the obligation) to change your course of action at some point of time in the future.

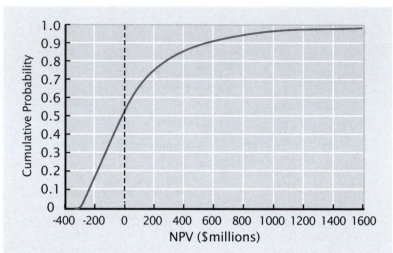

Figure 11.4. NPV for Project X

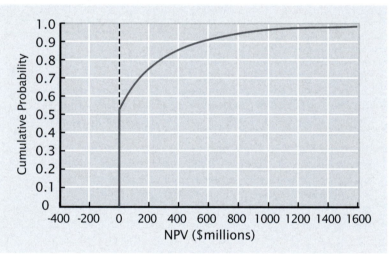

Figure 11.5. NPV for Project X With Exit Clause

Such options can be very valuable. The ability to wait until some time in the future to make a major decision greatly increases the likelihood of making the correct decision, and therefore greatly increases the likelihood of a profitable outcome. It's like being allowed to wait until halftime to decide which team you're going to bet on in a basketball game.

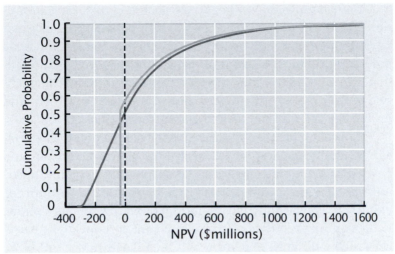

Figure 11.6. NPV for Project X With Exit Clause (Cost: $30 mm)

As an example, consider Figure 11.4. This is the cumulative probability curve for the NPV of a project under consideration. The EV of this curve (i.e., the mean) is $100 million, but there's a lot of uncertainty here. The p_{10} is a loss of $224 million, while the p_{90} equals a positive $544 million.

Suppose you could negotiate an exit clause – one that would allow you to abandon the project at some future date if you had indications that you were likely to be in a losing situation. What would that be worth?

The answer is illustrated in Figure 11.5. The original curve's downside is now limited to prevent it from going negative, assuming that under such circumstances, you would exercise your exit clause. The new EV is $175 million – quite an improvement! So you should be willing to pay up to $75 million for an exit clause like this one.

(For simplicity's sake, this example assumes that when the time comes for you to decide whether or not to exercise the clause, you have perfect information about the NPV of the project. This would not be the case, of course. In reality there would still be some probability that you would mistakenly get out or mistakenly hang in there. But the concept is the same.)

Say you are able to negotiate such a clause for $30 million. Figure 11.6 shows the comparison between the original project and the project with the exit clause for which you have paid $30 million. The original project has a p_{10} of –$224 million, a p_{90} of $544 million, and an EV of $100 million; the modified project has a p_{10} of –$30 million, a p_{90} of $514 million, and an EV of $145 million. Which would you rather have?

This example is simple but it illustrates a point. The typical deterministic discounted cash flow NPV calculation and related financial measures (like return on investment, internal rate of return, and profitability index) fail to account for value that can be added by including flexibility in one's plans. A deterministic NPV calculation assumes a specific future: revenues will be X, expenses will be Y, cash flows will be Z. Many projects – especially large, long-term projects – are significantly undervalued by a standard NPV calculation. Even a Monte Carlo analysis of NPV doesn't address option value (although it does account for risk and uncertainty). You have to build the model with the internal logic necessary to reflect future decisions, and before you can do that, you must identify what those future decisions might be.

DA is a wonderful process for understanding and capturing option value that often exists in our projects. We identify uncertainties and decisions that can have a large impact on the profitability of a venture, focus management attention on those issues, and then encourage creative thought regarding mitigating the downside and increasing the probability of realizing the upside. The strategic plans that result capitalize on these options and yield greater value for the company.

Following the Plan

Once an optimal approach is selected, all that remains is to implement the strategy. I say this with my tongue planted firmly in my cheek. There is nothing trivial or easy about implementing a plan. Business is littered with examples of good plans that were poorly executed. In fact, objectives, strategies and plans must be constantly revised, revisited, and re-

Howard Head's Skis

Howard Head, the inventor of the aluminum "sandwich" ski, is often cited as the ultimate example of the entrepreneurial spirit. In 1947, Mr. Head – an honors graduate of Harvard University and a gainfully employed engineer at the Glenn L. Martin Aircraft Company – took $6000 in poker winnings and rented a corner of an electrical appliance shop in Baltimore.[1] Six months later, he produced his first pair of skis and quit his job.

But when tested by ski instructors in Vermont, the skis broke. So did his next prototype. And the next. And the next. Thirty-nine prototypes and almost three years later, Howard Head had run out of his own money, run out of all the money he had borrowed, hadn't been paying his men for eighteen months, and was living in a $20/month basement apartment. He is quoted as saying, "Either this ski was the right one, or I would simply have to close down the business and go out and get a job."

Of course, the next ski *was* the right one, and the rest is history. Skiing changed forever, Mr. Head went on to revolutionize tennis as well, and retired in 1982 a multi-millionaire.

So was Howard Head talented, determined, or lucky? I would argue that he was all three. He was a creative engineer, and no one can doubt the spirit and determination of a man who spends three years and all of his own funds working on a project that repeatedly disappoints him. He earned every penny of his millions through hard work and intuitive brilliance.

But what if the fortieth prototype *hadn't* worked? What if financial reality had finally forced Mr. Head to go back to a nine-to-five job *before* he found the magic formula? Would we still laud him as an entrepreneurial genius? Almost certainly not. We probably wouldn't even know his name. And yet, he would have been the same imaginative, resourceful man. He just wouldn't have been rich and famous.

This is not to denigrate Mr. Head in any way – his reputation for intuitive insight and persistence is extremely well-deserved. My point is that there are many creative minds out there, inventing new and sometimes better ways of building things and doing things. Some of them – not many, but some – may very well have the same kind of ingenuity and dogged determination that Mr. Head had. But given the hit-and-miss nature of experimentation, very few manage to achieve their breakthrough before the threat of bankruptcy or penury drives them back into the rat race. In the entrepreneurial world, talent and fortitude just make you a player in the game. A little luck is almost always needed to win.

communicated. This is an iterative process – yesterday's "Can Wait Until Later" Decisions become today's "Focus" Decisions. The decision maker needs to be continually informed of the team's progress and planned course of action.

Further, implementation of the project – and indeed, the decision-making process itself – often requires careful change management. A good DA process requires a different way of thinking and communicating by everyone from the technical specialists to the executive decision makers. Expecting everyone to adapt smoothly is unrealistic. It takes time for companies to modify their processes and behavior. But the potential gains make it time well spent.

This decision process is the context in which probabilistic analyses must be done. Analysis for analysis' sake is a waste of time. The whole point of characterizing uncertainty, modeling it, understanding it, and gleaning insight into the key issues that create and destroy value on your projects is to *make better decisions*. If you already know what to do and cannot imagine new information changing your mind, don't waste your time re-examining the data – just do it and concentrate on execution. This notion will be treated in more detail in the next chapter, which focuses on the value of information.

Points to Ponder

What are some of the key change management issues associated with implementing a consistent decision process throughout an organization?

At what levels of the company would you expect to encounter the most resistance and how might you overcome this resistance?

Endnotes

1. Leuthner, Stuart. "A Bad Skier's Revenge," *Invention and Technology*, Winter 2004.
http://www.inventionandtechnology.com/xml/2004/3/it_2004_3_feat_0.xml

"Knowledge is of two kinds. We know a subject ourselves, or we know where we can find information upon it."
– Samuel Johnson

12

How Much Is That Data in the Window?

Many executives mistakenly believe that information always adds value. It is easy to convince ourselves that if we could only get our hands on enough data, we could make our decisions with confidence. Sometimes this is true; often, it is not. Information is almost never perfect. Even if we test our prototype or survey our customers, there is some probability that we will get erroneous or misleading results. In this chapter, we show how to determine whether information has value in a given situation, and how to estimate that value. We also explore the value of control – i.e., how much you should be willing to pay to control or influence the outcome of an uncertainty, rather than just to gain information about it.

The Value of Information in an Imperfect World

Much of the discussion so far has centered on how to use probabilistic methods when a major decision or set of decisions has to be made. For example, if you are planning to develop and produce a new product, you have to decide how big a factory to build, how to get the product to market, what the best market is for the product, etc. We've assumed that these decisions must be made now (or soon) with the information available.

But this is rarely the case. We often have another decision to make: Should we spend time and money to acquire new information to help us make the decision? If so, how much should we be willing to spend? Market surveys, additional clinical trials, expert opinions on the political stability of the country in which we're building a factory – any or all of these might enable us to make a better decision on a multi-million-dollar project. But all of these activities take time and cost money. How do you know if it is worth it to take the extra time and spend the extra money?

There is a straightforward approach to answering this question, usually involving something called a Bayesian transformation (named after Thomas Bayes, the 18th-century English mathematician who figured out how to calculate these things). A decision *analyst* needs to know how to calculate a Bayesian transformation, but the decision *maker* does not (provided he trusts the analyst). The decision maker just needs to be aware of the *nature* of value-of-information calculations.

The value of any piece of information is actually very simple: it is the difference between the expected value of the project (or asset, or portfolio) *with* the information and the expected value *without* it. The Bayesian transformation is just a tool for calculating that difference.

As a manager, you need to be aware of a number of issues regarding the value of information:

1) Information has value ***only*** if you would potentially alter a decision based on the information that you obtain

(like whether or not to invest in a new project, or what size plant to build). If you would do nothing different regardless of what you learn from the new information, it has no value.

2) Information that would cause you to make a different decision only under circumstances that have a zero or near-zero probability of occurrence has no value.

3) Corollary to Number 1: By itself, *increased confidence* has no economic value. Therefore, information that does nothing more than increase confidence in the decision you intend to make has no economic value. Note that I say *economic* value. If your corporate culture and/or reward system punishes you for a poor outcome, increased confidence that you are making the right decision may be worth quite a lot to you, personally. But it is worth nothing to your shareholders.

4) Corollary to the corollary above: If the cost of information exceeds the calculated value, you are better off deciding without it, *regardless of how uncertain you are*. Many corporate dollars have been squandered on additional data and/or analysis because a manager didn't have the nerve to make a tough decision in the face of uncertainty. It is easy to fall into an almost endless cycle of acquiring more data, doing more analysis, discovering that the new analysis still doesn't resolve the uncertainty, and therefore acquiring still more data. This just postpones an uncomfortable decision while creating the appearance of doing something about it.

5) Perfect information is exceedingly rare. There is usually some chance that the information you receive will be wrong (and/or it will be interpreted incorrectly).

6) The value of perfect information (however rare it might be) can often be calculated, and this number is useful. It represents the absolute maximum amount you should consider paying to acquire information (and only if it's extremely good information). You should almost always pay less than the value of perfect information.

7) The value of imperfect information can sometimes be estimated, depending on how much we know about the reliability of this information. When this calculation is done, it yields a better (and always lower) estimate of the maximum amount you should be willing to pay for the information.

8) If your company is in the business of searching for something very rare (a blockbuster new anti-cancer drug, a hit Broadway play, a low-carbohydrate beer that has flavor), then even extremely reliable information needs to be thought about very carefully. It might not be telling you what you think it is telling you. This is illustrated in the "Deadly Disease" scenario below.

9) The value of information increases with:

   ♦ the probability of making a wrong decision without any new information
   ♦ the cost of being wrong (including lost opportunity costs), and
   ♦ increasing reliability of the information.

The following two scenarios are presented to illustrate the concepts listed above. The first (the *Deadly Disease*) is a fun, somewhat qualitative exercise. The second (regarding opening a video rental store) is more realistic, rigorous, and quantitative. If it's been years since you had statistics and you'd rather hire someone you trust to do your calculations for you, skip the second one. Just be sure you understand the nine principles listed above before you leave this chapter.

The Deadly Disease

Imagine that a terrible new plague called stochasticitis is going around. It strikes its victims at random. However, it's rare: only one person in a million has it.

There is a very good blood test to determine if an individual has stochasticitis. If someone has the disease, 99% of the time, the test results will be positive (i.e., 1% false negatives). If someone does not have the disease, 99% of the time, the result will be negative (i.e., 1% false positives).

You take the blood test, and the test result comes back positive. *What is the probability that you actually have stochasticitis?*

I usually present this quiz near the beginning of my courses, and then give a prize at the end to the person who comes closest to the actual answer (sorry, no prizes come with this book). Usually, most of the answers are way off, but sometimes a few come close.

The easiest way to look at this problem is to imagine that 100 million random people take the blood test, and that statistics work perfectly.

Of the 100 million people, how many would actually have stochasticitis? One hundred, of course (statistics are working perfectly, remember, and one person in a million has the disease). The other 99,999,900 would be fine.

Of the hundred who have the disease, ninety-nine would test positive, and one would show a false negative. Of the 99,999,900 who are healthy, 999,999 (1%) would show a false positive, and the other 98,999,901 would test negative (see Table 12.1).

When you get your test result, all you know for sure is that you're one of the 1,000,098 who had a positive result – i.e., you fall somewhere in the first column of the table. But of those 1,000,098 people, only 99, or 0.009899%, actually have stochasticitis. Therefore, despite your positive test result, the probability that you have stochasticitis is only 0.009899%, or 1 in 10,102 (by the way, you just did a very simple Bayesian transformation).

Does this mean that the blood test yields no real information? Certainly not – a one in 10,102 probability is two orders of magnitude higher than a one in a million probability, which was your best estimate before the test was done.

Does it mean the information has no value? Possibly. Remember – in order for information to have value, *it has to cause you to change a decision* under at least one scenario. I

100 Million People Tested	Number of Positive Test Results	Number of Negative Test Results	TOTALS
Number With Disease	99	1	100
Number Without Disease	999,999	98,999,901	99,999,900
TOTALS	1,000,098	98,999,902	**100,000,000**

Table 12.1. Stochasticitis Chart

can't speak for anyone else, but discovering that I now had about a one in ten thousand chance of having a disease, rather than one in a million, would not be enough to make me rush out and spend my retirement fund on a new Ferrari.

The lesson to learn is essentially this: if whatever you're looking for is very rare, interpret imperfect information very cautiously. In such a case, even a very small percentage of false positives is likely to vastly outnumber the true positives (because true positives are so rare). So if you've run a television sitcom pilot past a focus group, and the group laughs uproariously and tells you they love it, be careful. That's good news, to be sure, but hit television shows are rare, and focus group reliabilities are often moderate at best. The probability that you have, in fact, found the next *Friends* is small.

The Video Rental Store

The previous brain teaser is fun and yields non-intuitive results. But while it uses Bayesian processes, we did not calculate the value of information.

The following exercise involves a real value-of-information (VOI) calculation, albeit in a very simple, hypothetical example. If the math is confusing, just skip this example and go back and review the nine points at the beginning of the chapter. It is not important for you, the decision maker, to know how to perform such a calculation, but it is important that you understand the principles involved.

High-speed VOI

VOI analyses need not be time consuming. They can often be done very quickly with rough numbers and still yield valuable results.

A major oil & gas company wanted to run a new logging tool in an appraisal well on a recent offshore natural gas discovery. The tool would give the company a better idea of how much gas was likely to be recovered (the key uncertainty), and therefore, what size development would be needed (the key decision). Two vendors offered somewhat different versions of the tool, but one had been field tested and was considered more reliable. However, using the more reliable tool would cost about $500,000 more than using the cheaper one.

They called me at about 10:00 a.m. to see if I could help them decide whether the added reliability of the information gained from the superior tool was worth the extra expense. They had to make a decision by the end of the day, U.K. time (I was in Houston). We set up a teleconference for noon (6:00 p.m. in the U.K.).

Fortunately, several of the gentlemen involved were comfortable generating rough estimates for the Expected Values of the project under the different scenarios on the Bayesian decision tree (i.e., different combinations of facilities sizes and recoverable quantities of natural gas). Even though we did not have time to generate precise estimates, we were able to work with numbers that everyone felt were of the right order of magnitude.

Yet even with these rough estimates, the result of the analysis was crystal clear. If the superior tool increased the probability of making the correct decision on the size of the facilities by just *one percent*, the Expected Value of the project increased by a million dollars – twice the incremental cost of the tool. Even when we went back and changed the input scenario EVs substantially, the indication was always to go with the more reliable tool. Despite a lack of hard data, the client could make this decision with confidence.

We were done by 2:00 p.m. Houston time.

Suppose you are considering opening a movie rental store near the entrance to a new housing subdivision. You estimate that the $p_{10} - p_{90}$ range for rentals per week is 1000 – 3000. Your analysis also indicates that if you are in the 2200 – 3000 rentals/week range, the store will be profitable. If you are in the 1000 – 2200 rentals/week range, the store will not be profitable and you will not pursue the opportunity. You currently believe that there is about a 40% chance that the demand

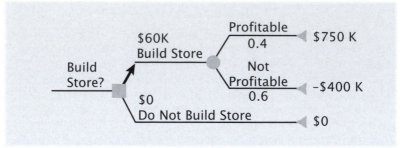

Figure 12.1. Initial Video Store Rental Decision Tree

will be in the 2200 – 3000 range and the store will be profitable.

If the store is profitable, the mean of the NPV curve is $750,000 (you're a good businessman, and you've done your analyses probabilistically). If you build the store and it is not profitable, the mean NPV is –$400,000. The decision tree, therefore, looks like Figure 12.1 (in decision trees, decisions are marked with squares, and uncertainties are marked with circles).

In this case, the logical choice is to build the store, because the expected value ($60,000) is greater than the value of walking away ($0). The EV is just the probability-weighted average of the different possible outcomes: ($750K x 40%) + (–$400K x 60%) = $60K. There are no probabilities associated with decisions – we get to choose one path or the other.

But this is hardly a compelling case. If there are any other attractive opportunities, you would probably pursue them first. Even without other opportunities, a $60,000 project may very well not be worth the time.

However, suppose you have the opportunity to conduct a marketing survey of the houses in the new subdivision to get a better idea of whether the rentals are likely to exceed 2200/week. This would be very useful information – *if* the information is reliable enough.

You estimate that if, in fact, the rental rate will be greater than 2200/week, there is a 90% probability that the survey would indicate so (and a 10% probability that it would erroneously indicate a rate of less than 2200/wk). If, in fact, the rental rate will be less than 2200/week, there is only a 75% probability that the survey would indicate so, and a 25% chance of erroneously indicating a rate of greater than 2200/wk (people often tell market surveyors what they think the surveyors want to hear).

So there are four possibilities:

♦ The rate would really be >2200/wk and the survey tells us so (probability = 0.4 x 0.9 = 0.36)
♦ The rate would really be >2200/wk and the survey erroneously says it would be <2200/wk (probability = 0.4 x 0.1 = 0.04)
♦ The rate would really be <2200/wk and the survey tells us so (probability = 0.6 x 0.75 = 0.45)
♦ The rate would really be <2200/wk and the survey erroneously says it would be >2200/wk (probability = 0.6 x 0.25 = 0.15)

The Bayesian probability table looks like Table 12.2. It shows that if we run the survey, the probability that it will indicate a good market (rentals >2200/wk) is 51%, even though our estimate of the actual probability of a good market is only 40%. This is because marketing data are not perfect. In this case, there's an asymmetry to the reliability of the data (we expect more false positives than false negatives).

If the survey does indicate a good market (which it will do 51% of the time), it will be correct 71% of the time (0.36/0.51 = 0.71) and incorrect 29% of the time (0.15/0.51 = 0.29). Likewise, if the survey indicates a poor market (which it will do 49% of the time), it will be correct 92% of the time (0.45/0.49 = 0.92) and incorrect 8% of the time (0.04/0.49 = 0.08).

Your decision tree is now more complex, as you have two decisions to make: first, you have to decide whether to do the marketing survey; second, you have to decide whether to build the store. Figure 12.2 shows this new tree, along with the appropriate probabilities and NPVs.

Probabilities of Different Scenarios	Survey Indicates Rentals >2200/wk	Survey Indicates Rentals <2200/wk	TOTALS
Actual Rentals >2200/wk	0.36	0.04	0.40
Actual Rentals <2200/wk	0.15	0.45	0.60
TOTALS	0.51	0.49	**1.00**

Table 12.2. Marketing Survey Reliability

The values on a decision tree are calculated backward, from right to left. At every uncertainty node (the circles), the calculated value is the probability-weighted average of the values of the branches. At every decision (the squares), we get to choose one path or the other, and we're assuming that we'll always choose the path of higher value. The bottommost path – "Just build the store without the marketing survey" – has the same NPV as the tree in Figure 12.1 ($60,000).

The tree shows that the value of the project is much higher with the marketing survey than it is without the survey ($212K vs. $60K). This extra value comes from avoiding building an unprofitable store some percentage of the time. The value of the information gained from the marketing survey is the difference between these two values: $152,000. If the survey costs less than this (which it almost certainly would), you should go ahead and acquire it; if the survey costs more, you are better off making your decision without it (which, as we have seen, would mean going ahead and building the store).

If, in the absence of any new information, you would not build the store, then the information gained from the survey has even more value. If you would walk away from this opportunity today, then the lowest branch of the tree in Figure 12.2 has a value of $0, not $60,000. The VOI is still the difference between the value of the project with the information and the value without it, but now the value without it (to you)

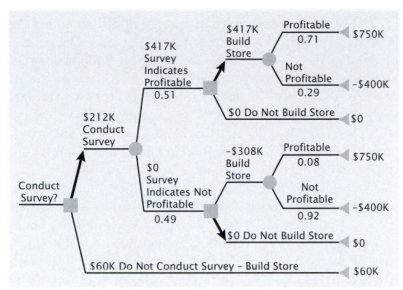

Figure 12.2. Decision Tree for Market Survey and Building Store

is $0. Therefore, the value *to you* of the information gained from the survey is $212,000. $152,000 of this is the inherent value of the survey. The remaining $60,000 is the additional value the survey has specifically for you because of your reluctance to pursue the project (despite its positive expected value). The survey convinces you to proceed with the project when circumstances are promising.

Not only does the survey add value, it greatly decreases the probability of substantial loss. Suppose Businessman A doesn't bother with probabilities and VOI analyses, but rather just demands "the number" from his subordinates. In this case, that number would be $60,000 – but that would be the average of a 40% probability of gaining $750,000 and a 60% probability of losing $400,000.

Compare that with Businesswoman B who examines the results of the VOI analysis and decides to conduct the survey. Not only does Businesswoman B have a much higher Expected Value ($212,000, less the cost of the survey), she also has a much lower probability of losing anything more than the cost of the survey. Recall that the probability of an end node of a decision tree is the product of the probabilities along the branches. So (ignoring the cost of the survey for now), the probability that Businesswoman B will lose $400,000 is just 15% (51% x 29%), compared with 60% for Businessman A. The probability that Businesswoman B will conduct the survey and then walk away is 49%, and the probability that she will gain $750,000 is 36% (51% x 71%). The cost of the survey buys her a much higher probability of making the correct decision, and a much lower probability of serious loss.

In reality, of course, the possible results would be a continuous range of values, from disaster to break-even to wild success. But the value of the information still holds – it would greatly improve your probability of making a good decision, thereby increasing the EV of the project. Breaking the continuous distribution into discrete parts for the purpose of evaluation doesn't change this.

In this scenario (whether you would pursue the project with no new information or not), the value of the information is significantly higher than the likely cost of acquiring it. However, cases in which the value of information is marginal or zero are common, too. When considering whether to acquire information, people often fail to take the reliability of the information fully into account. They think, "If we get this information and it tells us that the situation is A, we'll do B." The correct line of thought is, "If we get this information and we interpret the situation to be A, what is the probability that we're correct?"

Many managers mistakenly believe that more information is always better (and technical personnel often hold this belief even more strongly than do managers). This is not always the case; sometimes, you're better off making the decision now, despite the uncertainty.

The Value of Control (VOC)

Look again at Figure 12.2. It tells you that conducting a marketing survey adds about $152,000 in value to your planned video rental store by giving you a better idea of how likely it is that the people in the new subdivision will rent enough videos for you to be profitable.

But what if you could do more? What if you could not only find out about people's intentions regarding renting videos from your store, but could actually *make* them rent these videos? What would that be worth?

You cannot really do this, of course, but you can certainly influence potential customers. It's called advertising. Advertising doesn't guarantee increased business, but it usually improves the odds. How much might good advertising be worth in this case?

Our best information today says that if we average more than 2200 rentals per week, the expected value of the new store is about $750,000. So if we could somehow guarantee a high rental rate, we would expect the venture to have an NPV somewhere in this neighborhood. Compare that with our current estimate of the expected value of the store ($60,000) and we can estimate the absolute maximum value added by a top-notch advertising campaign ($750,000 − $60,000 = $690,000 added value).

You should never pay this much, of course. First, if you paid this much and got your high rental rate, you would just be breaking even relative to where you would be if you proceeded without any advertising; the cost of the advertising would negate the value of the added revenue. But more importantly, no advertising is perfect, and what we've estimated is the value of *control* (VOC), not the value of *influence*. Influence is worth less than control, but at least we now have a boundary point from which we can scale back to what we think the advertising is really worth.

The best way to look at it is from the point of view of probabilities. VOC is the value associated with changing our current estimate of the probability of a high rental rate to 100% (it was 40% in our original assessment). Control *guarantees* that we'll have a successful venture.

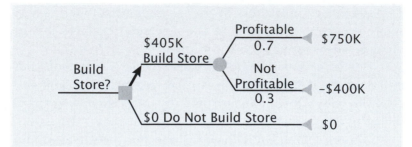

Figure 12.3. Advertising Increases Probability of Profitable Store

As we've already noted, advertising doesn't guarantee anything, but should improve our odds. Let's say we estimate that a good advertising campaign will increase the probability of a successful store from 40% to 70% (Figure 12.3). Our new expected value for the store is $405,000 [($750,000 x 70%) + (–$400,000 x 30%)]. This is $345,000 more than the expected value of the store without a big advertising campaign. We should be willing to pay up to this amount for the campaign (although, again, if we pay this full amount, we just break even relative to our base case; we should be paying less).

This is quite a bit more than the $152,000 we estimated a marketing survey to be worth. This is to be expected; actually getting people to rent videos from your store is worth more than just finding out if they intend to do so.

However, the very act of conducting the survey would help to advertise the new video rental store – so the survey would not only have informational value, but also some control (or at least advertising/influence) value. It might be worth considerably more than our initial estimate of $152,000.

So VOI and VOC analyses sometimes have a gray area of overlap between them. This complicates matters somewhat, but not too badly. We just need to make sure we've considered *all* the potential benefits associated with the activity/survey/ etc. we're evaluating. Most of the time, we don't have to get the value estimate exactly right; if it comes out to be significantly higher or lower than the cost, the decision to proceed is easy.

The Overlap Between VOI and VOC

One of my clients was recently considering implementing new processing machinery technology. The key uncertainty was how reliable the new design would be. The client wanted to know whether to proceed with a staged deployment, or to build a test (or pilot) version first to get some idea of how often the new machinery would break down once it was implemented.

However, building a test version would not only give *information* about reliability – it would also allow the design team to *increase* the reliability of the second generation machines. This proved to be a crucial point. The estimated Value of Information was zero, but the Value of Control was hundreds of millions of dollars. Even if the client realized only a fraction of the full VOC value, the test version of the machinery would be well worth the money.

It is important to look for both values – information *and* control.

Fighting Analysis Paralysis

People hate uncertainty. People who have to make decisions involving large sums of capital *really* hate uncertainty. But in today's volatile business world, you have to make most decisions without knowing what is going to happen. This can be stressful for a typical manager who is trying to invest the company's money wisely without taking any undue risks. Under these circumstances, the temptation to run one more survey, to acquire a bit more data, or to wait until a competitor's intentions become apparent can be enormous. We think if we could just get our hands on enough information, we could make this decision with total confidence.

This is often called "analysis paralysis." The fact is, uncertainties are unknowable. No amount of data collection or analysis is going to tell you what the price of steel will be in two years, what your market share will be after your product launch in Japan, or when China will decide to allow the Yuan to float freely against other currencies. Spending inordinate amounts of time and money trying to pin things down too precisely is often just a subconscious stall tactic. We do it because we're not comfortable committing the company to a major investment in the face of high uncertainty – which is a perfectly logical discomfort to have. But it doesn't add value to the company.

Value-of-information and value-of-control calculations are a good way to cut through this web of tentativeness. They cannot eliminate uncertainty, but they can show us when it makes sense to spend time and money on new information and when it does not. From there, it's just a matter of gathering one's nerve and making a decision.

I need to give a similar warning about the opposite situation. If you've already decided what to do, if there is no way that you're going to change your mind, don't waste time and money acquiring more information. A basic tenet of VOI analysis – indeed, of all decision analysis – is if you know what you're going to do, just go ahead and do it. Analysis of any kind only has value if the decision maker will seriously consider multiple alternatives.

A lot of information has been presented in this section. If this has been too much detail for you, just go back and review the nine points at the beginning of the chapter. As the decision maker, these are the key concepts with which you should be familiar. The rest is just math, and can be left to a trusted analyst.

Points to Ponder

Usually uncertainty can be mitigated in one of four ways:

♦ Gather more information and perform more analyses.
♦ Plan, negotiate, and/or design for flexibility and options to allow for future decisions to be made as uncertainties are resolved.
♦ Create a portfolio of assets with enough independence (or, better yet, negative correlation) to reduce the uncertainty to an acceptable level on a percentage basis.
♦ Offload the risk onto a third party (i.e. hedge or buy insurance, which is paying someone to take the risk for you).

What are the advantages and disadvantages of each of these approaches?

Valuing Flexibility: The Flip Side of the Value of Information

An automobile manufacturer faced a nagging question: how much flexibility should they build into their assembly lines? Most lines could be set up to assemble a fixed mix of vehicles, but once set up, re-tooling for a different vehicle mix was time-consuming and costly. The lines would be set up optimally for the pre-launch sales forecast, but whenever the sales forecast was off – and sometimes it was way off – the inflexible mix resulted in shortages of popular vehicles and "holes" in the assembly lines of slower-selling vehicles.

The manufacturer had a new technology to enable the assembly lines to switch flexibly from model to model, but implementing this technology would be expensive. They wanted to know whether they should make this investment.

This is actually a problem of information. If one could know ahead of time which vehicles would sell well, one could optimize the lines with confidence at the time of vehicle launch and be done with it. The problem is that predicting the behavior of the buying public has never been easy. No matter how good your marketing research, no matter how many surveys you take, you are never going to get it *exactly* right. And sometimes you're not even going to be close!

The next-best thing to knowing ahead of time is being able to react quickly once you do find out. This is flexibility, and it can be worth quite a lot.

Our vehicle manufacturer was lucky. They had decades of sales data, including records of orders for popular models that went unfilled because the assembly lines couldn't keep up with demand. They were able to go back and estimate how much more profitable the company would have been had they been able to fill every order.

The result was staggering: over the years, billions of dollars in profit had been lost due to the perennial mismatch between what the public wanted and what the assembly lines could deliver. It was well worth the investment to install flexibility into the lines to meet this demand.

In the absence of historical data of this type, one must estimate the probabilities associated with various levels of sales for different products. It's imperfect, but if you're honest about what you don't know, you can still get an idea of how much value flexibility might hold for you.

In the deterministic world, however, it is almost impossible to estimate the value of flexibility. You always believe your forecast because – imperfect as it may be – it's the best you have.

"What if this is as good as it gets?"
– Melvin Udall, played by Jack Nicholson

13

Optimization and the Efficient Frontier

We have introduced and discussed a number of useful stochastic tools. In this chapter, we introduce two more: optimization and the efficient frontier. These are especially useful in complex situations involving multiple strategic decisions and competing objectives. At the portfolio level, multiple goals are common – if nothing else, we want to maximize expected returns and minimize the probability and magnitude of potential loss. This is the appropriate level at which to consider these competing objectives and try to strike a good balance.

Back in Chapter 11, we defined (among other things) uncertainties, decisions, facts, and objectives. Let's take another look at these four facets of business.

If you are dealing with a situation in which there is very little uncertainty (i.e., all of the input parameters are essentially facts) and you have only one major decision to make, then a deterministic analysis is usually all that is required. Unfortunately, this is usually the case only with relatively minor, day-to-day decisions. Longer-ranging, strategic concerns are more complex.

So we add a layer of complexity. If you have uncertainties, a Monte Carlo simulation (or maybe several simulations) should help to provide the insight you need to make a good decision. Several companies make excellent off-the-shelf Monte Carlo simulation software that rides on top of Excel, so this level of modeling is relatively easy to implement. You don't have to build new models; you can modify your existing spreadsheet models.

However, major projects usually involve several strategic decisions, not just one. This was discussed in Chapter 11 when we covered Decision Analysis (DA). A new product launch, for instance, might involve deciding:

♦ How many geographic areas in which to introduce the product
♦ Which specific areas
♦ Whether to launch simultaneously or sequentially
♦ How much of the new product to produce the first year
♦ How rapidly to ramp up production
♦ Whether or not to build a new plant to manufacture the product
♦ How much to spend on advertising
♦ What type of advertising.

If you have uncertainties *and* several significant decisions to make on an asset or project, then you're really looking for that *combination* of decisions that will yield the optimal result. You want to find the *strategy* that maximizes some measure-of-value (e.g. the highest mean NPV) within the constraints you have to deal with (a budget of X million dollars) while meeting any other requirements the company may have (no more than a 5% chance of losing money). You now require an optimization. (From a business process perspective, you're once again into the world of Decision Analysis, which we covered briefly in Chapter 11. The purpose of DA, after all, is to find the optimal path forward. The optimizers described in this chapter are excellent tools for jump-starting this process.)

Optimization involves running hundreds or even thousands of Monte Carlo simulations, varying the input decisions each time, and comparing the key statistics of the output curves.

In the product launch example, we might initially launch in the northeastern U.S. and Europe simultaneously, position the product as a cheaper alternative to the current market leader, ramp up production rapidly, and spend heavily on television advertising in both markets. We then run the simulation, and store the NPV output curve.

We then try a different set of decisions – maybe launching in the entire U.S. but not Europe, and focusing our advertising on magazines – re-run the simulation, and compare the new output curve with the first one. If it's better, we throw out the first one and replace it with the second. Note that "better" will depend on which statistic we've chosen to compare, and what constraints and requirements we've put on the model. If we're optimizing mean NPV, and the mean NPV is higher in the second simulation, and all of our requirements and constraints are met, the new curve is declared "better."

This process is repeated thousands of times if necessary, but unlike each individual Monte Carlo simulation, the process is not random. Trying every possible combination of decision values could, in some cases, literally take years. Besides, there's nothing random about decisions; there are no probability curves because we *choose* what we will do. Therefore, a good optimization program learns as it goes along, and hones in on those combinations of decisions that hold the most promise for optimizing the value of interest. In this manner, the optimization program eventually finds that set of decisions that will optimize our desired metric within our constraints and requirements.

At this point, most managers cry foul. "No machine is going to make my decision for me! I may look at what it has to say, but I'm going to make the ultimate decision here!" I could not agree more. None of these analyses – Monte Carlo simulation, decision trees, optimization, or efficient frontiers (about which we will talk in a moment) – let you off the hook for actually making the decision, and none of them are going to make the decision for you. As cliché as it sounds, they're just tools. Very good tools, but tools nonetheless.

So when your optimizer comes back and says that the set of decisions from simulation Z yielded the best results, you need to dig a little deeper. First, is there another simulation that came close to Z's results, but is less risky? Within the constraints you set, the software will simply optimize the statistic you give it. There may be another set of decisions that yields a slightly lower mean NPV but with less downside risk. Make sure you look for these things.

Second, how resilient are the recommended decisions? Look at the results that come within 5% or 10% of the best run. Which choices appear in nearly all of these simulations? If a certain choice for a certain decision shows up in nearly all of the best results, that hints at a winner – a choice that is likely to be good regardless of which specific course of action you pursue. On the other hand, if a certain decision displays a number of different choices in the top 5% or 10%, this tells you two things:

- ♦ the choice made in the top-rated optimization is probably not a resilient choice, and
- ♦ this specific decision doesn't appear to have a major impact on the optimized measure-of-value.

As such, if you prefer a different alternative, you can choose it.

Of course, you can make different choices for the resilient decisions, too – after all, you're the boss. But you should have a good reason for choosing what may turn out to be a sub-optimal alternative. Perhaps you have another priority or objective that wasn't included in the original model.

Which brings us to efficient frontiers. If, on top of your uncertainties and multiple decisions, you also have several different objectives, you should build an efficient frontier to show the tradeoffs between satisfying one objective vs. another. Multiple, conflicting objectives are the norm, not the exception, if for no other reason than we want to 1) maximize return on investment, and 2) minimize risk.

Efficient frontier theory comes from portfolio management. If a portfolio is a possible combination of investments, then there is an infinite number of different portfolios available to us. We can invest in different combinations of stocks, government bonds, real estate, money market funds, precious metals, oil wells, baseball cards, racehorses – the list is endless.

For every one of these portfolios, we can calculate the expected return on our investment and we can calculate the risk. (Even though I'm using the term, "calculate," these figures would be based on uncertainties – probability distributions – for most of the inputs. Therefore, the expected return would be the mean of the output curve).

Recall that different industries define risk in different ways.

♦ In the financial world, the most commonly accepted definition of risk is beta – the degree to which the value of the individual investment (or in this case, portfolio) correlates with the value of the market as a whole over time (the "market" being the set of *all* available investments – not just publicly traded stocks).

♦ Other industries use value-at-risk (VAR) calculations to estimate risk.

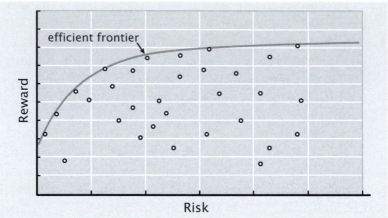

Figure 13.1. The Efficient Frontier

♦ Still others equate risk to the variability of the expected return (often the standard deviation of the output value distribution).

But regardless of how risk is defined, it can be calculated. If you then plot all of the possible portfolios of investments on a Reward vs. Risk graph, you'll get something like Figure 13.1 (every circle is a portfolio).

Efficient frontier theory says that you should consider only those portfolios of investments that lie along the upper-left boundary of your collection of points (the curved line). Why? Well, consider any other point in the collection – say, the circled point in Figure 13.2. For the exact same level of risk, you could move up the vertical arrow to another portfolio with a higher expected value. Or you could get the exact same expected value with a much lower level of risk by moving to the left along the horizontal arrow. So why would you ever choose the circled portfolio? Quite simply, you wouldn't. The only portfolios worth considering are those that lie along the upper-left boundary – the efficient frontier. (Pop quiz: what portfolio is represented by the point where the efficient frontier intersects the y-axis on the left? That's right – 100% U.S. T-bills).

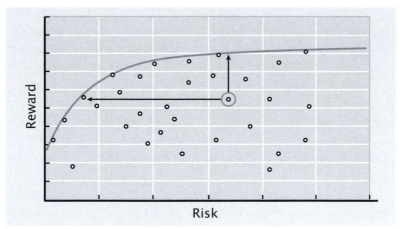

Figure 13.2. An Inefficient Portfolio

The curvature seen along the heavy line in Figures 13.1 and 13.2 is typical of reward-vs.-risk efficient frontiers. At low levels of risk, small increases in risk result in substantial increases in expected return. However, as you move to the upper right along the frontier, it becomes harder and harder to achieve higher levels of return without taking on a large amount of additional risk.

So let's get back to our optimization process. Optimizers can only optimize one thing at a time. Conflicting objectives are handled as *requirements* on certain statistics (other than the one being optimized). For example, if we want to maximize the mean NPV, but we also want to have no more than a 5% chance of losing money on the project, we would put a requirement in the optimization process that the p_{05} of the output NPV curve must be greater than zero. Thus, any simulation run in which the p_{05} NPV is negative would automatically be thrown out, regardless of how high the mean NPV might be. Problem solved: the optimization program shows you the result with the maximum mean NPV, but only considers those results that have at most a 5% chance of losing money.

But this creates a new problem. Suppose an opportunity were to present itself that had a 6% chance of losing money, but had twice the expected NPV of the best simulation run that met the 5% hurdle rate. Would you take it? Of course you would. Such a huge increase in expected value in exchange for such a small increase in risk is a great tradeoff.

But if you've put a requirement into the model that the p_{05} NPV must be greater than zero, you're not even going to see this opportunity. The program will screen out all results that fail the requirement, and your twice-the-mean-NPV set of decisions will be thrown out before you get a chance to look at it.

What should you do? The answer is to run multiple optimizations, each with a different set of requirements. So instead of drawing a line in the sand at a 5% chance of losing money, you find the optimal decision set with that level of risk, then find the set of decisions that optimizes your result with no greater than a 6% chance of losing money, then a 7% chance, etc. This can take a while, but eventually, the optimization software will plot these results on a graph and you can see the reward vs. risk tradeoff for yourself (see Figure 13.3). The software builds the efficient frontier. You can then decide what degree of risk you're comfortable with, and choose the optimal combination of decisions for that level of risk.

Again, you wouldn't blindly proceed based only on the simulation results. Once you decide which part of the efficient frontier represents the best return for the risk, you examine the output from that optimization more closely, looking for resilient decisions, critical decisions, irrelevant decisions, etc. – all the things we talked about earlier under optimization.

Portfolios are dynamic beasts (in fact, the word comes from the Latin *portare*, meaning "to carry", which implies movement).[1] You are unlikely to choose a collection of investments in January and then make no changes during the rest of the year. You are almost certain to drop some of them, pick up new ones, get new information, etc. It is better to have a portfolio comprised of projects and assets that are likely to remain good choices when combined with any of a wide range

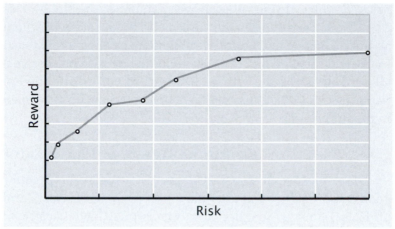

Figure 13.3. Efficient Frontier from Multiple Optimizations

of other investments – i.e., resilient projects and assets – than to include projects and assets that generate a good reward/ risk portfolio only when combined with specific other investments.

Efficient frontier analysis is not limited to the tradeoff between reward and risk. The two axes can be any two objectives that conflict (or partially conflict) with each other – e.g., short-term cash flow vs. long-term value creation (this tradeoff is emphasized in Michael Allen's book). Once managers realize that efficient frontiers are an excellent way to examine and quantify tradeoffs between objectives, they often identify new potential applications.

Portfolio management is just a special case of optimizing a set of decisions. Whether you're planning an individual project and have a number of decisions to make (like the size of a manufacturing plant, the location, how flexible to make the design, etc.) or you're managing a portfolio of assets and must decide which assets to include and which to exclude, the optimization and efficient frontier concepts are the same.

However, the distinction between these two types of optimizations is fuzzier than I've presented in the previous paragraph. In reality, portfolio management is integrated with the strategies planned for each individual asset, and those strategies should be tied in with the overall business portfolio strategy. It's an iterative thought process. The question of which assets to include and exclude will depend on the plan for each asset, and the plan for each asset should be based on the overall portfolio strategy, with an eye toward optimizing the entire portfolio (which usually does not mean optimizing each individual asset).

Go for the Gusto, or Play It Safe?

You may recall that in Chapter 5, I made the case for adopting a risk neutral attitude when evaluating assets and projects – that is, judging each opportunity based solely on the Expected Value (the probability-weighted sum of all possible outcomes). You should also recall that this recommendation came with a very large condition: on any one asset or project, you have to be able to afford to lose. If a single project is so large that its failure could cause serious problems for the company, you obviously cannot base your decisions solely on the EV. You must also consider the probability of failure occurring, and weigh the EV against the probability of financial distress. Your fiduciary responsibility requires no less.

The same thought process applies at the corporate portfolio level (which is the ultimate "big project"). You're talking about the entire company here. If you lose at the portfolio level, you may go out of business. Therefore, the "best" return for the risk depends heavily on your tolerance for potential loss – or rather, the tolerance of your shareholders and creditors. This doesn't preclude investing in individual projects that are far riskier than your shareholders would go for. It just means that when these projects are incorporated into the portfolio, the overall level of risk has to be acceptable to those who have provided the capital. The portion of the efficient frontier you ultimately choose at the portfolio level should reflect your investors' tolerance for uncertain returns and potential losses.

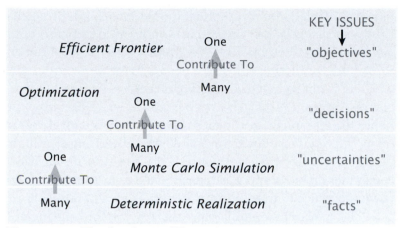

Figure 13.4. The Stochastic Hierarchy

So let's recap. Generally, there are four types of issues identified in the decision analysis process: facts, uncertainties, decisions, and objectives. Figure 13.4 shows one way to look at the relationship between each of these types of issues and the level of analysis needed in any given situation:

♦ If you have nothing but facts and a single decision to make, a deterministic analysis will do.

♦ If you have uncertainties, but still a fairly straightforward decision to make, use a Monte Carlo simulation to gain insight before deciding.

♦ If you have uncertainties and a number of key decisions to make (but a fairly unambiguous objective), perform an optimization (which is just a large number of Monte Carlo simulations).

♦ If you have uncertainties, multiple decisions, and several conflicting objectives, create an efficient frontier, showing the tradeoff between the conflicting objectives. This is done by running multiple optimizations.

This hierarchy is not a universal truth; it is a simplification. Real-world situations often fail to fit neatly into a single level of the hierarchy. You might have multiple objectives but very little uncertainty, in which case an efficient frontier built using multiple runs of a deterministic model might clarify things sufficiently. You might have only one significant decision – maybe go/no go on a major project – but loads of uncertainty and conflicting objectives between partners. Often, the problem is not so much conflicting objectives as it is *ambiguous* objectives – either the boss hasn't made clear what he hopes to accomplish, or the message has been misinterpreted along the way. Once the team sits down, talks things through, and agrees what they're trying to do, the way forward becomes clear (this is another reason you'll hear so much about the importance of framing in Decision Analysis courses).

The hierarchy simply represents a way of relating the issues raised in the decision analysis process with the different types of analytical tools available so you can choose the tools that are appropriate for the situation.

I want to emphasize this point. The decision making process – and the tools used – need to be customized and scaled to each situation. This is a statement of the obvious, but decision analysts can get into trouble by trying to apply the full-blown process (and all of the tools) to each situation, regardless of complexity. When scaled and applied correctly, the process actually reduces the time to arrive at a robust and optimal plan of action, as well as vastly increasing the chances of developing an optimal plan in the first place. It is a matter of knowing the process, being familiar with the tools, and understanding the outputs of the analyses.

Points to Ponder

We have discussed reward vs. risk and long-term value creation vs. short-term cash flow as two examples of competing objectives. What is important to consider when balancing these two objectives? What are other examples of competing objectives?

Endnotes

1. Bill Haskett pointed this out to me years ago.

"A single death is a tragedy, a million deaths is a statistic."
– Iosif Vissarionovich Dzhugashvili, a.k.a. Joseph Stalin

"Statistics are no substitute for judgment."
– Henry Clay

"I hate statistics. What I got to know, I keep in my head."
– Jerome Hanna 'Dizzy' Dean

14

Dangerous Curves Ahead – Statistical Quirks and Traps

We have all heard that "there are lies, damned lies, and statistics."[1] There are many ways that statistics can fool us – some innocent, some not so innocent. Just as Monte Carlo simulation can be used for Machiavellian purposes, so, too, can almost any statistical data. As a decision maker, you must keep your wits – and your skepticism – about you. This is not a justification for ignoring statistical results; rather, it is a mandate to truly think about them.

In this chapter, we'll discuss two common misunderstandings that occur when people do not understand how statistics behave. There are other examples as well, but these two will suffice to get the point across. Sometimes these misunderstandings arise because of non-intuitive characteristics of certain statistical measures. Sometimes they arise because someone is intentionally manipulating your opinions and decisions. In either case, it pays to be aware of the numbers' quirks – it might help you to avoid some common traps.

The Trap: Believing that Improbable Equals Impossible

A number of years ago, I attended a seminar sponsored by an oil and gas service company specializing in seismic data acquisition and processing. Computing power had made the extraction of complex seismic attributes (I won't bore you with what those are) much easier, and these could be cross-plotted against various rock properties (like porosity, thickness, etc.) as measured in oil and gas wells that had been drilled.

The seminar speaker advocated a shotgun approach: just cross-plot every seismic attribute against every rock property. If a cross-plot shows a strong correlation (say, 0.90 or 0.95), you can be fairly sure that that seismic attribute is a good indicator of that rock property in that geologic basin.

I would have left the seminar but for the fact that I had carpooled with a colleague. The seminar speaker was promoting a very dangerous approach to the interpretation of statistical correlations. An example may help to show why.

The Super Bowl has been played every year since 1967. Those of you who have enough gray hair and are American may remember that the first four games were between the National Football League champions and the American Football League champions. After the 1970 game, the two leagues merged into one league (the National Football League) with two conferences: the NFC and the AFC, whose champions would meet in the Super Bowl every year. In order for the two conferences to have the same number of teams, three NFL teams moved over to the AFC: the Cleveland Browns (now called the Baltimore Ravens), the Baltimore Colts (now the Indianapolis Colts), and the Pittsburgh Steelers (who are, incredibly enough, still the Pittsburgh Steelers).

From 1967 through 1997, if the original NFL or (after 1970) NFC, or one of the three ex-NFC teams mentioned above won the Super Bowl, the Dow Jones Industrial Average went up that year. If an AFL or AFC team won (except for the three teams mentioned above), the Dow went down. This held true 29 times in 31 years – an incredible 93.5% success rate for this obviously overlooked market indicator!

The odds of this happening by chance are approximately one in one hundred million. And yet, can anybody doubt that it is, in fact, pure coincidence? How can the winner of the Super Bowl possibly have any effect on the stock market? It doesn't, of course – this correlation is just an amazing coincidence. It's improbable, but not impossible, for this to have happened purely by chance.

The Super Bowl/Dow Jones correlation is an amusing example of a highly improbable occurrence that nevertheless occurred, but it also demonstrates the need to think critically about apparently undeniable correlations. Modern computing power has made it possible to cross-correlate data, trends, statistics, etc. on a massive scale. While this is a boon to researchers (and those of us who benefit from their research), it also greatly increases the opportunity for bogus interpretation of statistical results.

Nowhere is this more apparent than in the field of medical research. Once upon a time, a researcher had to formulate a hypothesis (say, that smoking increases the probability of getting lung cancer), collect and analyze data on the subject, determine if there is a correlation within the data, and determine whether the correlation is statistically significant (which is done by calculating the probability that the correlation could have occurred by random happenstance, like the Super Bowl example).

Does Watching Oprah Cause Stress?

Self-help author Hale Dwoskin was investigating theories concerning causes of stress when he decided to conduct a survey.[2] Of 1015 people polled, 5% called themselves "super-stressed." Of that 5 percent, 50% called themselves fans of Oprah Winfrey – a much higher percentage than one would expect from a random sampling of people. Does this mean that stressed-out people are more likely to watch Oprah? Does this mean that watching Oprah stresses people out? Hardly. The correlation is almost certainly spurious – and meaningless.

Today, it is possible to dispense with the first part of this process – the hypothesis – and proceed directly to data collection and analysis.* Hundreds of lifestyle traits can be cross-correlated with hundreds of illnesses. Lo and behold, one of them shows a strong correlation! And the probability of this correlation occurring at random is only one in 15,000! It *has* to be significant!

Well, no it doesn't. Cross-correlating, say, 100 illnesses with 150 totally unrelated lifestyle traits will not result in 15,000 zero correlations. Rather, you'll get a normal "bell curve" of correlation values, with most of them clustered near zero, but a few values out in the tails, near 1 and –1. So let's say your cross-plot of Listening to Barry Manilow Music vs. Developing Alzheimer's Disease shows a correlation of 0.98, and the analysis says that the odds of this happening by chance are one in 15,000. You can point to the 15,000 cross-plots and say, "One in 15,000 – yes, that makes sense – here are 15,000 cross-plots, and here's the one that – totally by chance – shows an extremely high correlation. It could easily be a statistical anomaly." (But then again, it *is* Barry Manilow....).

---

*I'm not saying that all or even most medical research is conducted in this way. The vast majority of medical researchers do, indeed, formulate hypotheses prior to collecting data. But those data are often then cross-correlated along multiple dimensions in ways never before possible, creating a huge opportunity for spurious results to be erroneously interpreted. It is likely that this has contributed to the number of studies in recent years that produced "statistically significant" results, only to have subsequent studies fail to replicate those results.

Therefore, don't put your critical thinking aside when faced with statistical data – even apparently overwhelming statistical data. There are more than six billion people in the world, each of whom engages in dozens of activities every day. There are bound to be "incredible" coincidences occurring all the time. If neither you nor the smartest people you know can figure why two apparently correlated items should share a dependency, the correlation is likely anomalous (and meaningless). Don't fall into the trap of believing that there has to be a reason (logical or divine) for every highly improbable event that takes place.

The Trap: Selective Statistics

A commercial by a major insurance company aired on January 4th, 2004 during the Sugar Bowl game in which Louisiana State University defeated Oklahoma for a share of the US collegiate national football championship (my wife attended LSU, so this was a joyous day in our household). The commercial argued that oftentimes, the premiums charged by Company Y (the company whose ad it was) were lower than those of many "discount" insurance companies.

The ad had the following line (this is a paraphrase, but the facts are correct): "Nearly 7 out of 10 people who switched [to Company Y] saved an average of $200 by switching."

At first pass, this seems impressive; after all, if I could save $200 a year on my insurance premiums without sacrificing any coverage or service, I'd certainly make the change. But upon closer examination, these data have been seriously culled.

First, Company Y is limiting the analysis to those people *who decided to switch to them*. Now ask yourself, why would somebody decide to switch? Usually to save money. So it should come as no surprise that these people ended up saving money. What you don't know (because Company Y did not disclose it) is how many people made the comparison and decided *not* to switch, or worse yet, decided to switch from Company Y to some other insurer. For all we know, the vast majority of people fall into this category but have been left out of this analysis.

Second, there's the "nearly 7 out of 10" phrase. This isn't like the "7 out of 10 doctors recommend..." quote that we hear so often, in which the statistic of interest is the *percentage* of doctors who prefer some brand. The statistic put forward here is the *average*. If the figure being presented is an average, shouldn't it be the average of the entire study group? Why leave out 3 of every 10 people? So not only is Company Y limiting itself to those who decided to switch, it is throwing out some 30% of those people – the bottom 30% in terms of savings, I'm willing to bet – before calculating the "average" savings. Figures like these perpetuate the adage that there are "lies, damned lies, and statistics."

If a statistic is loaded with qualifiers and limitations, warning bells should go off in your head.

I could fill an entire book with examples of misleading statistics, but other than amusement, there isn't much point. Everybody knows statistics can be misleading. Conflicting data are common, especially when we are inundated with a flood of unfiltered – and sometimes unreliable – information, as we are today. My purpose is to show a couple of examples of how and why this confusion occurs, and more importantly, to encourage you to think critically about statistical data that just don't seem to make sense.

However, there is a world of difference between "doesn't make sense" and "doesn't say what I thought it would" or "doesn't say what I want it to say." In a recent *Harvard Business Review* article, Jeffrey Pfeffer and Robert Sutton make a strong case that far too many business managers don't pay *enough* attention to hard data, but rather base their decisions on conventional wisdom, personal experience, and anecdotal evidence.[3] Please do not interpret this chapter as a green light to reject any analysis that yields non-intuitive, unexpected, and/or unwelcome results. I'm encouraging you to think critically about the information you receive, not to ignore it. I could fill another book with examples of leaders who rejected perfectly sound analysis and excellent recommendations because of their own biases, preconceived notions, and closed-mindedness, and as a result, blundered badly. Blind faith in numbers is no better or worse than blind faith in one's own beliefs and opinions.

Points to Ponder

Consider the following statements:

♦ "The best mileage of any vehicle in its class."
♦ "The first game is critical – 67% of the time, the winner of the first game goes on to win the series."
♦ "97% fat free!" (as seen on a package of lunch meat)
♦ "It is the network with the fewest dropped calls – an independent survey proves it."

How might the purveyors of these messages be using "selective statistics?" What information are they *not* giving you?

Endnotes

1. Courtney, Leonard Henry, 'To My Fellow-Disciples at Saratoga Springs,' *The National Review* [London] 26 (1895) 21-26 at page 25.

2. Article in the Houston Chronicle Nov. 19, 2003, by Josh Shaffer of Knight Ridder Tribune News.

3. Pfeffer, Jeffrey, and Sutton, Robert I. "Evidence-based Management," *Harvard Business Review*, Vol. 84, No. 1, pp. 63-74, 2006.

"Shallow men believe in luck."
– Ralph Waldo Emerson

15

Final Thoughts

I don't believe that Emerson meant to dismiss luck entirely. Shallow men *rely* on luck. They naively hope for good fortune to compensate for their own lack of effort and thought. Shallow men fail to make contingency plans. They convince themselves that their own forecasts for the future somehow represent what *will* happen, not just what they would *like* to have happen. They cannot think probabilistically and don't know how to plan for multiple possible outcomes.

Anyone who refuses to *believe* in luck is denying reality. I have seen hard-working, intelligent people undone by events nobody could have foreseen. I have seen people of mediocre talent who happened to be in the right place at the right time become very successful. To deny that randomness plays a huge role in this world is folly. And yet there is a tendency among business people to invoke luck only when trying to explain how their well-thought-out plans could have gone awry. "The price of our basic input materials jumped 40% in two months

– no one could have predicted that!" Rarely does one hear, after a record-setting quarterly income statement, "If the baht hadn't plunged 70% relative to the yen, we would have lost our shirts. We really got lucky this time!"

Talent, dedication, and ability are obviously important. However, you need to expend at least some energy attempting to understand the uncertainties and random processes that affect your life and livelihood (especially when you know that there are talented, dedicated competitors who are doing their best to understand *their* key uncertainties). By doing so, you can best position yourself to take advantage of opportunities when they arise and possibly avoid catastrophes that might befall a less prepared individual. You cannot always eliminate the possibility of a bad outcome, but you can often reduce the probability and/or the magnitude of that outcome. This usually makes the difference between superior long-term results and mediocrity.

I cannot emphasize this point too strongly. Many executives believe that their job is to examine the available information, pick the brains of the smartest people they can afford to hire, and make a determination regarding the future. Then they implement a corporate strategy that will be successful under the predicted scenario.

This is a good start, but we can do better. By all means, gather pertinent information (although gathering data is relatively easy today – separating the meaningful from the irrelevant is the challenge). Hire the smartest people you can afford, even if – no, make that *especially* if – they disagree with you on key issues.*

*The Value of Diverse Perspectives

In the immortal words of Dee Hock (the man who transformed Bank Americard into the trillion-dollar consumer credit powerhouse that is Visa), "Never hire or promote in your own image. It is foolish to replicate your strength. It is idiotic to replicate your weakness. It is essential to employ, trust, and reward those whose perspective, ability, and judgment are radically different from yours. It is also rare, for it requires uncommon humility, tolerance, and wisdom." (as quoted in "The Trillion-Dollar Vision of Dee Hock," *Fast Company*, October-November 1990, p. 5).

But develop *scenarios*, not *a scenario*, for the future. There are always multiple possible futures, some more probable than others. A good corporate strategist identifies those outcomes with the highest probability of occurrence and devises a plan that will position the firm to thrive under any of them. By planning for multiple scenarios, you enable your firm to change quickly if the world changes from one scenario to another. You can only do this if you truly understand the key uncertainties that drive value in your business.

At this point you should have a pretty good overview of probability theory and statistical analysis as they apply to business in today's uncertain world. But analysis by itself accomplishes little. Any probabilistic analysis has to be done within the context of a solid decision-making process. Probabilistic analyses won't give you "the answer," but they will help you to gain insight and understanding about the decisions that need to be made.

Decision makers must understand these tools if they are to be used beneficially. You should understand how they work (at least on a macro level), what their strengths and weaknesses are, and what the outputs mean.

I encourage you to reject the "Why can't you just give me the number?" mentality and to take the plunge into probability ranges and curves. They contain far more useful information than do individual numbers.

Decision makers must also understand their own strengths and weaknesses as human beings trying to grasp counter-intuitive ideas. There is nothing natural about the idea of Expected Value, especially when the probability of actually realizing that particular value is essentially zero (or in some cases, literally zero). There are times when our intuition about an uncertain situation will lead us down dangerous paths. We need to be alert to these situations and find the essential balance between rational and emotional thinking.

The combination of a solid grasp of probabilistic methods and executive-level strategic business skills is extremely powerful. These are two sides to the gold coin of competitive advantage, the tangible and the intangible, the analysis that can be taught and the instinct that cannot. A management team that views the world clearly through a probabilistic lens and brings top-notch business acumen and experience to the table is a force to be reckoned with.

Consider a final quote from R. Richard Ritti: "Leaders do make a difference in the success of organizations. On the other hand, good fortune bears an uncanny resemblance to good judgment" (Ritti, page 140).

When you are unsuccessful, try to separate the effects of random variance from actual trends that you might have been able to foresee. Don't expect to win every hand. Like a good poker player, focus on the *decisions* you've made (rather than the outcomes of those decisions), and learn from your mistakes. You may have simply been unlucky, but I wouldn't immediately jump to that conclusion – it resembles rationalization and abdication of responsibility.

When you are successful, enjoy it – but stay humble. You might just be out at the tip of the bell curve of random variance. It's a nice place to visit, but only the very lucky get to live there.

Bibliography

Allen, Michael S., 2000. *Business Portfolio Management: Valuation, Risk Assessment, and EVA™ Strategies*. New York: John Wiley & Sons, Inc.

Bernstein, Peter L., 1998. *Against the Gods: The Remarkable Story of Risk*. New York: John Wiley & Sons, Inc.

Kahneman, Daniel, and Tversky, Amos, ed., 2000. *Choices, Values, and Frames*. Cambridge, U.K.: Cambridge University Press.

Kujawski, Edouard, and Alvaro, Mariana L., 2004. *Quantifying the Effects of Budget Management on Project Cost and Success*. Presented at the Conference on Systems Engineering Research, University of Southern California, Los Angeles, 15-16 April, 2004.

Natemeyer, Walter E. and McMahon, J. Timothy, ed., 2001. *Classics of Organizational Behavior, 3rd ed*. Prospect Heights, Illinois: Waveland Press Inc.

Nutt, Paul C., 2002. *Why Decisions Fail: Avoiding the Blunders and Traps that Lead to Debacles*. San Francisco: Berrett-Koehler Publishers, Inc.

Ritti, R. Richard, 1998. *The Ropes to Skip and the Ropes to Know: Studies in Organizational Behavior, 5th ed*. New York: John Wiley & Sons, Inc.

Skinner, David C., 1999. *Introduction to Decision Analysis, 2nd ed*. Gainesville, Florida: Probabilistic Publishing.

Taleb, Nassim Nicholas, 2001. *Fooled by Randomness: The Hidden Role of Chance in the Markets and in Life*. New York: Texere LLC.

Winkler, Robert L., 1972 and 2003. *An Introduction to Bayesian Inference and Decision, 1st and 2nd ed*. 2nd Edition Gainesville, Florida: Probabilistic Publishing.

Glossary

(These are not necessarily the definitions one would find in a statistics text. I have tried to use laymen's language to describe what these terms mean specifically in the world of business risk management. Where a more detailed discussion of the term can be found in the text, I have given a page reference).

Ambiguity: A lack of clarity in meaning.

Certain Equivalent (CE) [page 50]: The amount that an individual is willing to take (with 100% certainty of receiving it) in exchange for the right to a project or deal in which the return is uncertain. The CE is often given as a percentage of the Expected Value of the uncertain deal. For example, if an individual has the right to roll a standard die and receive $10 x the number that comes up, the Expected Value of the deal is $35. If that individual would take $28 in exchange for the deal, her CE is 80% ($28/$35).

Contingent Probability [page 71]: A probability of occurrence that is dependent on the outcome of another event.

Continuous Distribution [page 27]: A probability distribution or histogram in which any value within the range is possible.

Correlation [page 26]: A mathematical relationship between two sets of data which indicates the probability that a dependency exists between the parameters underlying the two data sets and the strength of that dependency. Example: if you were to plot the heights versus the weights of a thousand randomly selected individuals, you would find a strong correlation between the two parameters. Knowing the value of one parameter gives you an idea about the value of the other.

Critical Path [page 110]: The string of tasks or sub-projects that determines the overall time it will take to complete a project.

Cumulative Distribution, also called "S-curve" [page 28]: Values are plotted along the x-axis and the probability of occurrence of a value *less than or equal to* the given x-value is plotted along the y-axis. The y-axis, therefore, goes from 0 to 1.

Decision [page 124]: An irrevocable action that commits resources to one course of action or another.

Decision Analysis (DA) [page 128]: A process through which companies and teams can gain insight into the key issues that drive value on their projects and in their business. This enables them to confidently develop and choose strategic alternatives that have higher probabilities of achieving their objectives.

Decision Tree [page 33]: An analysis tool in which several discrete values are used to represent the range of possibilities for each uncertainty, and several different alternative choices are modeled for each decision to be made. The "tree" is then built from left to right, with each uncertainty and/or decision appearing in chronological order. Probabilities are assigned for each branch of each uncertainty, and Expected Values are assigned for each "terminal node" at the right-hand edge of the tree. The value is then calculated from right to left, with probabilities applied at each uncertainty node and the optimal path chosen at each decision node.

Dependency [page 26]: Dependency refers to a real-world relationship or connection between two factors. Example: the price of aluminum depends on the quantity of bauxite mined.

Deterministic [page 5]: Using single values for each input parameter and generating single values for each output calculation.

Discrete Distribution [page 27]: A probability distribution or histogram in which only certain values within the range are possible.

Efficient Frontier [page 163]: A curve showing those strategic alternatives that offer the highest value as pertaining to one objective, given different requirements regarding another, competing objective. Thus, an efficient frontier shows the trade-off between satisfying one goal and satisfying another goal.

Expected Value (EV) [page 34]: See "Mean."

Frequency Distribution [page 27]: For discrete output distributions, a chart plotting values along the x-axis and the probability of occurrence for each value along the y-axis. For continuous output distributions, a histogram in which the x-axis is divided into a large number of "bins" of equal size and the y-axis shows the probability of occurrence of a value within any given bin.

MAIMS Effect (Money Allocated Is Money Spent) [page 119]: The phenomenon that the money used to complete a project or task will never be less than the amount allocated for that project or task.

Mean [page 86]: The probability-weighted average of all values in an output distribution. The mean is the Expected Value (EV) of the distribution.

Measurements of Central Tendency [page 86]: The mean, median, and mode. One of these three statistics is commonly selected to represent an entire distribution.

Median (also called the p_{50} value) [page 86]: That value in a probability distribution about which there is a 50/50 probability of the parameter coming in higher or lower.

Mode [page 86]: The value in a probability distribution that has the highest probability of occurrence.

Monte Carlo Simulation [page 38]: A process in which a probability distribution is given for each of the inputs to some algorithm (say, one that calculates NPV), and then a computer runs the algorithm many times (usually hundreds or thousands of times). On each trial, the computer selects a different value for each input parameter, honoring the range and probability distribution given for that parameter. Thus, the computer generates a different value for each output of interest (say, NPV) on each trial. At the end of the simulation, a histogram for each output of interest is created from the list of possible values that has been generated, and statistics are calculated for that list.

Net Present Value (NPV): A representation of the current value of a future net cash flow stream. Each value in the stream is discounted back to today using an appropriate rate (usually the weight-adjusted cost of capital, or WACC).

Objective [page 124]: A goal.

Optimization [page 161]: A process through which the combination of decisions that maximizes a key measure-of-value (within certain constraints) is derived.

$p_{10}/p_{50}/p_{90}$ [page 16]: The values corresponding to the 10th, 50th, and 90th percentiles, respectively, of a probability distribution.

Probabilistic: See "Stochastic."

Probability Distribution [page 8]: A curve or histogram showing the range of possible values for the parameter in question along the x-axis and the probability of occurrence (or relative probability of occurrence) along the y-axis.

Risk (defined as it is used in this book) [page 8]: Where used as a noun: the probability of loss times the potential magnitude of that loss. Where used as a verb: to take a chance; to put oneself in a position in which there is some probability of loss.

Risk Neutrality [page 47]: An approach in which each opportunity is evaluated based solely on its Expected Value, with no further consideration of the probabilities of success or loss.

"S" Curve: See "Cumulative Distribution."

Skew [page 30]: A term used to describe distributions that are not symmetrical about the mean. In a right-skewed distribution, the extreme values on the high side are farther from the mean than are the extreme values on the low side. In a left-skewed distribution, the extreme values on the low side are farther from the mean than are the extreme values on the high side.

Standard Deviation [page 86]: A commonly used measure of how wide a probability distribution is (i.e., how broad the uncertainty is), often represented by the symbol σ (sigma). Statistically, the standard deviation equals the square root of the variance.

Stochastic (also called Probabilistic, and often called Monte Carlo) [page 5]: Using a range of values and associated probabilities for each input parameter (usually given as a probability function), and generating a histogram of values for each output calculation (sometimes called an output probability distribution).

Tornado Chart (as used in sensitivity analysis) [page 30]: A chart which indicates the impact each uncertainty has on the measure-of-value of interest. These are extremely useful for determining which uncertainties have the potential to drive the value of a project up or down, and which ones can safely be ignored for now.

Uncertainty [page 8]: A parameter or measurement the value of which we do not know, and cannot know until some time in the future.

Value of Control (VOC) [page 152]: The increase in the Expected Value of a project or asset that comes from being able to control the value of a key uncertainty.

Value of Information (VOI) [page 142]: The increase in the Expected Value of a project or asset that comes from acquiring a certain piece of information.

Appendix

The Shell Game

Variations on this puzzle have appeared in numerous publications, often as the "Let's Make a Deal" problem or the "Monte Hall" problem (although the logic involved in that specific puzzle is actually significantly different and more complex than the one presented here). I include it in this appendix because brain teasers like this one are excellent exercises in thinking through a probabilistic problem. They may seem silly or academic, but breaking a situation down into all of the different possible outcomes and then assessing the probabilities associated with those outcomes is a great start on developing an optimal approach to solving the problem at hand.

The situation is this: The Prizemaster shows you three identical boxes, A, B, and C (Figure A.1). He tells you that two of the boxes are empty, but one of them holds a solid gold coin. This is not his coin; therefore, he has no motivation to

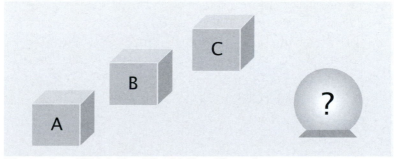

Figure A.1. Which Box Would You Choose?

help you, nor hinder you in your efforts to find the coin. He does, however, know which box holds the coin.

He tells you to pick a box. Completely at random, you choose box A. He then shows you that box B is empty (Figure A.2). This is the way he always plays the game – you choose a box, and then he shows you that one of the two remaining boxes is empty. He makes you an offer: you may keep box A, or you may trade it for box C.

What should you do? There are three possible answers:

♦ Keep A
♦ Trade for C
♦ It Doesn't Matter.

"It Doesn't Matter" invariably gets the most votes in my classes. The correct answer is "Trade for C." Why? Because the probability that you have the coin in your box – Box A – hasn't changed; it's still 33%. There is no dependency between this probability and the probability that the Prizemaster will show you an empty box – or to put it another way, the probability that the Prizemaster will show you an empty box is not contingent upon whether or not you have selected the box with the gold coin. Therefore, when the Prizemaster shows you the empty box, you have learned nothing new about the probability that your box holds the gold coin.

In order to understand this, let's contrast the Prizemaster puzzle with a slightly different scenario that yields a more intuitive result. Suppose that, rather than the Prizemaster

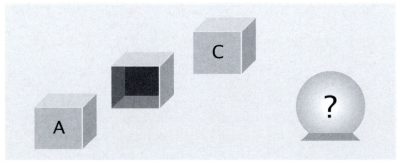

Figure A.2. Box B is Empty

choosing which box to reveal, a random person from the audience – someone with no clue as to where the gold coin is – comes up after you've chosen box A and gets to reveal either what's in box B or what's in box C. That person opens box B (at random). Box B proves to be empty. The Prizemaster now asks you if you would like to keep box A or trade it for box C.

Now what should you do? In situations like this, it helps to see what the event tree looks like for this sequence of events. An event tree is like a decision tree, except that the nodes are events that simply occur, rather than decisions that we make (technically, our selection of a box is a decision and the choice of which box to open by the person from the audience is a decision, but since both are random decisions, they can be treated as events). The event tree for the scenario with the random audience member appears in Figure A.3.

The first event in the tree is your selection of a box (box A in this case). After that event, there are two possibilities: either you have the gold coin, or the Prizemaster still has the gold coin. The probability that you have the coin is 33%, and the probability that the Prizemaster has the coin is 67%.

The second event is the audience member revealing what's in one of the Prizemaster's boxes. For each of the two branches of the tree, there are now two more branches: either the gold coin is revealed, or it's not. The probabilities associ-

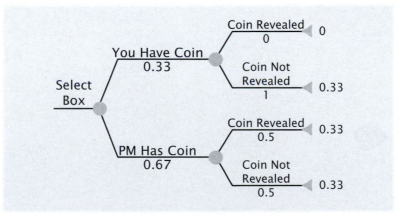

Figure A.3. Event Tree for Random Audience Member

ated with these branches depend on whether or not you have chosen the box with the gold coin; they are *contingent* on the outcome of the first event. If the gold coin is in box A (i.e., you have the coin), then the audience member will reveal the gold coin 0% of the time (after all, she's only allowed to open one of the Prizemaster's boxes), and the gold coin will remain hidden 100% of the time. If the gold coin is still in the Prizemaster's possession, then 50% of the time the audience member will reveal the gold coin, and 50% of the time, she will not.

We now have four possible end scenarios:

1) You have the coin and it is revealed.
2) You have the coin and it is not revealed.
3) The Prizemaster has the coin and it is revealed.
4) The Prizemaster has the coin and it is not revealed.

To calculate the probability of each of these end scenarios, we simply multiply the probabilities along the tree leading to that end branch. So the probabilities for each of the above scenarios are 0%, 33%, 33%, and 33%, respectively.

But you get a new piece of information: the audience member reveals an empty box! You can now safely eliminate all end scenarios in which the gold coin is revealed (scenarios 1 and 3 – see Figure A.4). The remaining end scenarios are

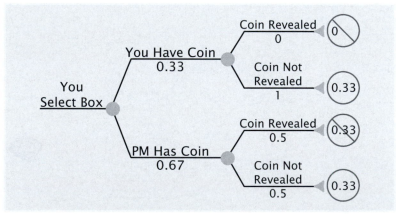

Figure A.4. Event Tree After Coin Is Not Revealed by Audience Member

now the only possible cases; therefore, the total of their probabilities needs to be normalized to 100%, and the new probabilities calculated. In this case, each of the two scenarios has a probability of 33%, so the new, normalized probabilities will each be 50%.

Therefore, it makes no difference whether you keep box A or trade it for box C – you have a 50/50 chance either way. So far, so good (and fairly intuitive).

Now let's look at the event tree for the original case – the one in which the Prizemaster (who knows where the gold coin is) reveals an empty box (Figure A.5). As you can see, this looks just like Figure A.3, but with one important difference: the probability of end scenario 3 – the one in which the Prizemaster has the gold coin, and the gold coin is revealed by opening one of his boxes – is 0%. This is because the probabilities associated with the second branches of the tree are *not* contingent on the outcome of the first branch; the Prizemaster knows where the gold coin is, and he is never going to show it to you; he is always, always, always going to reveal an empty box, because that's how the game works. The outcome of the second event is *independent* of the first. Therefore, the probability of end scenario 3 drops to zero, and the probability of end scenario 4 – the one in which the Prizemaster has the gold coin – is 67%. Which is exactly what it was before he revealed the empty box.

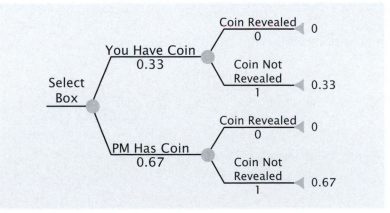

Figure A.5. Event Tree for Prizemaster

When the empty box is opened, the end scenarios that are eliminated – numbers 1 and 3 – both have probabilities of occurrence of 0% (Figure A.6). The remaining two scenarios have probabilities of 33% and 67%; they already total 100%, so they don't have to be normalized. The probability that the gold coin is in box C is twice that for box A. Therefore, you should definitely take the Prizemaster up on his offer, and trade box A for box C.

This specific situation is certainly contrived (I can't recall the last time someone gave me the opportunity to win a gold coin by picking a box). Nevertheless, the methodology used to solve this puzzle is applicable to more situations than you might think. You would be surprised at how many complex business situations can be clarified by simply sketching a decision tree to capture all of the events, uncertainties, decisions, and possible outcomes. We then consider the probabilities associated with each of the uncertain events, the information we are likely to gain along the way, and what it all means for the probabilities associated with the final outcomes. We can then make appropriate contingency plans for various future scenarios.

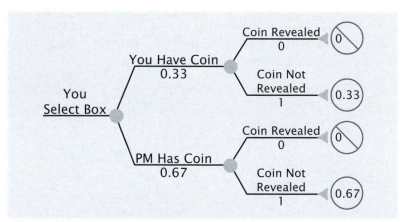

Figure A.6. Prizemaster Does Not Reveal Coin

Index